Learning Theories in
Childhood

Learning Theories in
Childhood

COLETTE GRAY *and* SEAN MACBLAIN

Los Angeles | London | New Delhi
Singapore | Washington DC

First published 2012
Reprinted 2012 (twice)

SAGE Publications Ltd
1 Oliver's Yard
55 City Road
London EC1Y 1SP

SAGE Publications Inc.
2455 Teller Road
Thousand Oaks, California 91320

SAGE Publications India Pvt Ltd
B 1/I 1 Mohan Cooperative Industrial Area
Mathura Road
New Delhi 110 044

SAGE Publications Asia-Pacific Pte Ltd
3 Church Street
#10–04 Samsung Hub
Singapore 049483

Library of Congress Control Number: 2011936468

British Library Cataloguing in Publication data

A catalogue record for this book is available from the British Library

ISBN 978-0-85702-145-8
ISBN 978-0-85702-146-5 (pbk)

Typeset by C&M Digitals (P) Ltd, Chennai, India
Printed in Great Britain by MPG Books Group, Bodmin, Cornwall
Printed on paper from sustainable resources

DEDICATION

This book is dedicated to my husband Norman, my lovely children and my beautiful grandson, Jacob.

Colette Gray

To my father James who first introduced me to the ideas of the philosophers and to my wife Angela and our children.

Sean MacBlain

CONTENTS

KEY TO ICONS

Chapter Aims

Summary

Recommended Reading

ABOUT THE AUTHORS

Colette Gray is Head of Research Development at Stranmillis University College, a College of The Queen's University of Belfast. She is a principal lecturer in Early Childhood Studies and a Visiting Professor (Child Development and Education) to University College Plymouth, St Mark and St John. A chartered developmental psychologist, she has studied and taught a range of aspects of child development for more than 20 years. Her research interests include the impact of special needs on the young child's learning, the ethical challenges involved in participatory research with young children, and gender and achievement. Married for 36 years, Colette recently became a proud grandmother to a beautiful baby boy. She looks forward to studying child development at close quarters within a new family generation.

Sean MacBlain is Reader in Child Development and Disability at University College Plymouth, St Mark and St John, where he has the research lead for the Centre for Professional and Educational Research. Sean worked previously as a Senior Lecturer in Education and Developmental Psychology at Stranmillis University College, a College of The Queen's University of Belfast. Prior to working as an academic, Sean worked as an educational psychologist and continues in this field in his own private practice. Sean's research interests include the professional development of teachers and early years practitioners and the social and emotional development of children and young people with special educational needs and disabilities. Sean is married to Angela and lives in Devon, England.

PREFACE

The idea for this textbook developed from our frustration with the lack of an available text of this type to recommend to students studying early years modules. At a time when university fees have tripled in some areas and course materials have become increasingly expensive, we believe it is essential for our students to have access to books which discuss a range of related theories in detail. With this in mind, contained within one text, we aim to introduce you to early philosophies of learning, the founding fathers/mothers of early years approaches and to key theorists from the behaviourist, cognitive and social interactionist traditions. You may note a new innovation here – the inclusion of behaviourism, a class of theories rarely referenced in other early years texts. This is largely due to the fact that many early years scholars do not accept this theory of learning. Yet, as you read, you will come to understand how it provided a springboard for further research into the development of learning and has informed behaviour management in the home, in early years settings and in the classroom. Indeed, so influential is this theory that we endorse the principles of this theory when we state 'behaviour has consequences'. It is not, however, our intention to argue in favour of any particular theory. On the contrary, we hope you will note the strengths and weaknesses of each approach and come to your own conclusions about their contribution to the body of knowledge on children's thinking and learning.

We realize that many students prefer to cherry pick rather than read a text in its entirety and, for that reason, employing a chronological approach, the strengths and weaknesses of each learning theory are highlighted to provide you with a comprehensive overview of, amongst others, behaviourism, cognitive constructivism, social constructivism and modelling theories of children's learning. We will bring the debate full circle to a discussion of the new social studies of childhood. Here we challenge current thinking by exploring the strengths and weaknesses of this approach. In the final chapter of this text, we consider the reality of learning theory in practice. This chapter also considers the role of reflection in improving practice. We hope you will find the examples provided informative and will complete the exercises included in each chapter. In particular, give careful thought to the exercise included in Chapter 1 and revisit your response to this question when you have read the theories discussed in the book. Have you changed your mind or do you remain firmly committed to one stance and, if so, can you support your theoretical approach with facts?

We have enjoyed writing this book. It has been challenging and thought-provoking and has enhanced our own understanding. We hope it will become a cornerstone of your learning and that it will enhance both your understanding of young children's learning and your practice.

AN INTRODUCTION TO LEARNING THEORIES

This chapter aims to:

- familiarize the reader with the organization and structure of the book
- provide a brief synopsis of each chapter.

We are convinced that learning begins at inception and continues throughout life. Although this approach is frequently termed cradle to grave, we believe that learning precedes birth as babies become familiar with sounds heard frequently during pregnancy, including the sound of their mother's voice. Hepper (1996) had a group of mothers relax after their evening meal and another group keep busy. He found the group who relaxed tended to watch a popular Australian television programme, Neighbours, which aired at around 6.30pm on most evenings. After birth, mothers in the relaxation group were able to settle their babies more easily when they played the Neighbours theme tune. Babies in the busy mothers' group showed no reaction to this tune. Hepper (1996) concluded that, prior to birth, babies in the relaxation group had learned an association between the Neighbours theme tune and relaxation. From birth onwards, babies are interactive processors of information. Some learning is incidental, effortless and undirected, whilst other learning is effortful, purposeful, directed, creative and reflective. For example, you might settle down to show a toddler how to put a jigsaw together (directed learning) but find their attention drawn to (incidental learning) an activity at the writing table. By the end of the session, the child might be able to tell you that 'S is a snake, a slithering snake' but have no clue how to put the jigsaw together. This situation reflects the sheer complexity of human learning. It suggests that learning can be affected by situational factors such as the presence of others, background noise, or internal factors such as tiredness or level of interest. Once learned, however, most information is permanently remembered. Examples of permanent skills acquired in early childhood include walking, talking, riding a bike and reading and writing. Simply stated, learning is the acquisition of knowledge and skills (David et al., 2011).

For more than 2000 years, philosophers, academics and educators have attempted to explain and define human learning. The Greek philosopher Aristotle (384–322 BC) believed that learning develops through repetitive exercises. According to Aristotle, the State must be charged with responsibility for instilling virtue, habits, nature and reason into children and for ensuring they became citizens of benefit to society. Almost a hundred years later, Socrates (470–399 BC) described learning as a process of remembering. He believed that all knowledge exists within the human soul before birth but, perhaps due to the trauma of birth, the soul forgets all it previously knew. Through a process of questioning and inquiry, termed Socratic dialogue, the soul recovers some aspects of knowledge.

Definition

Learning is the acquisition of knowledge or skill.

In contrast, Locke (1632–1704) argued against the existence of innate ideas (formed before birth), describing the child's mind as a *tabula rasa* or blank slate. Consistent with Aristotelian philosophy, Locke believed that knowledge is acquired through experience, repetition, training and virtue. He emphasized the importance of enjoyable learning and insisted that teaching should begin in early childhood. Locke's assertions were radical for their time but were shared by a number of influential thinkers including, amongst many others, Pestalozzi (1746–1827), Froebel (1782–1852), Dewey (1859–1952) and Montessori (1870–1952). Whilst each offers a unique insight into children's learning, importantly for our discussion these philosophers and educators have a shared belief in the importance of educating the young child.

Rousseau (1712–1778), for example, argued that education should follow the child's natural growth rather than the demands of society. His emphasis on the innate development of human nature became the primary philosophical basis for many alternative movements in education. In the early 1800s, the Swiss humanitarian Pestalozzi opened schools for orphans, based on Rousseau's principles. His work inspired educators in Europe and America. Froebel, a teacher at Pestalozzi's school, later became famous as the founder of the kindergarten concept. Montessori shared Froebel's belief that children should be taught social skills and empathy. While Froebel used creative and imaginative play to achieve his goals, Montessori employed real-world experiences such as cleaning a room, caring for animals, building a toy house or making a garden to develop these skills.

Dewey shared with Montessori and Froebel the notion that education should be child-centred, active and interactive; and that education must involve the child's social world and community. Influenced by the teaching philosophies of the early pioneers in the field of early childhood education, Dewey emphasized the importance of experiential learning and the process of teachers and children learning together. The teachings of the founding fathers and mothers of early childhood education are explored in greater detail in Chapter 2 where their unique contributions are highlighted. Similarly, the topic of experiential learning is given a more thorough analysis in Chapters 4 and 5 of this book as we explore the theories of Piaget (1896–1980) and Vygotsky (1896–1934).

It is, however, theories of learning which form the central foci of this book. The last century witnessed a significant shift away from philosophical propositions to the development of a range of empirical theories of learning; each claims to explain the origins of some aspect of learning. Before considering influential educational theories of learning, it seems appropriate at this juncture to define the word theory. In common usage, the term can be used to denote a set of statements or principles devised to explain a group of facts or phenomena, especially one that has been repeatedly tested or is widely accepted and can be used to make predictions about natural phenomena (Dorin et al., 1990).

> **Definition**
>
> A theory is a set of statements or principles devised to explain a group of facts or phenomena.

According to Woollard (2010, p. 472), a theory is 'an unproven conjecture or hypothesis that gives a tentative insight into a complex situation through to a well established explanation of that complex situation'. Darwin's Theory of Evolution, Maslow's (1943) Hierarchy of Needs and Gardner's (1983) Theory of Multiple Intelligence are examples of frequently referenced theories. Arranged in a five-stage hierarchical pyramidal format, Maslow, for example, posits that lower order physiological needs must be met before higher order needs can be satisfied. The first level in the hierarchy concerns basic physiological needs such as water, air, food and sleep; the second is about the need for safety and security; the third involves belongingness, love and affection; the fourth relates to the need for esteem, personal worth, social recognition and accomplishment; at the fifth level, the summit of the hierarchy, is self-actualization. According to Maslow, very few people reach this level but those who do enjoy moments of profound happiness and find deep fulfilment as they achieve their full potential. Maslow's theory provides a useful tool for understanding the factors that impede or progress learning. Nevertheless, it is unsurprising to find that even popularly known theories are the subject of criticism. Maslow's theory, for example, has been heavily critiqued for its lack of scientific rigour and for failing to acknowledge contradictory aspects of human nature. Moreover, it is unidirectional and fails to take account of individual priorities. By way of example, 18-month-old Kevin is a quiet child who rarely cries. Small for his age, Kevin is frequently hungry and sometimes searches for food in the bin. Kevin has learnt that it is better to go hungry (biological need) than to risk the slap that comes when he cries. Even at this young age, Kevin has learnt to prioritize his safety needs (level 2) over his biological need for food (level 1).

In essence, the theories included in this book will provide the reader with a general rule or principle about some aspect of learning. Each theory has strengths and weaknesses. We aim to highlight both and, where appropriate, to compare and contrast them. It is not our contention that one theory is superior to another, or that any single theory holds the key to learning, or even that any of the theories discussed are sufficiently developed to explain all aspects of human learning. On the contrary, we hope to engage the reader in a level of critical reflection that may cause them to accept or reject aspects of each theory. We believe that by studying the content of each chapter, examining the tables included and completing the tasks provided, the reader will develop a greater insight into the complexities of children's learning.

Chapter 3 introduces the theories of Pavlov (1849–1936), Thorndike (1874–1949), Watson (1878–1958) and Skinner (1904–1990). Each explored an aspect of learning underpinned by the principles of stimulus–response. For that reason, they are typically referred to as behaviourists. A branch of psychology, behaviourism remained a dominant force in education for more than fifty years. Although it lost prominence in the 1970s, behaviourism continues to have an influence on pedagogical practice in twenty-first century classrooms. Behaviourists believe that all behaviour, no matter how complex, can be reduced to a simple stimulus–response association. They focus on measurable outcomes rather than on introspective processes (imagery, feelings and thoughts, etc.).

In the course of his experimental research with dogs, the physiologist Ivan Pavlov noted that dogs salivated when laboratory technicians entered the room. Further research revealed the dogs had made an association between the technicians (neutral stimulus) and food (stimulus) and this caused their drooling response. Termed classical or Pavlovian conditioning, the theory was developed further by Watson who demonstrated classical conditioning in humans using young boys known as Little Albert and Little Peter.

Skinner extended Watson's stimulus–response theory to explain more complex forms of learning. He believed it was possible to use the principles underpinning animal experimentation with infants and children. He coined the term operant conditioning to explain the influence positive and negative reinforcers have on shaping and maintaining the child's behaviour. Skinner's theory continues to exert a direct and profound influence on education and is particularly evident in the reward and punishment systems teachers use to shape and maintain pupil behaviour. Star charts, praise, positive feedback and circle time are examples of popularly used positive reinforcers whilst time out is a negative reinforcer. The work of the social learning theorist Bandura (1925 to present) is included by some theorists in discussions on behaviourism (Woollard, 2010). Although he employed the experimental methods favoured by behaviourism, Bandura's inclusion of imagery, mental representations and reciprocal determinism (the child influences and is influenced by their environment) marked a radical departure from traditional behaviourist approaches. For that reason, his work is discussed in Chapter 6 alongside Bronfenbrenner's (1917–2005) social learning theory.

Chapter 4 considers the constructivist theory of learning. Though they continue to co-exist, this theory offers a considerable departure from that of behaviourism. Constructivism views learning as an active, constructive process with the child engaged at every stage. Rather than focus on measurement, cognitive theorists use observations and discourse analysis (interviews) to explain the development of internal cognitive processes. The term 'cognition' refers to internal mental processes and cognitive development to the acquisition of 'knowledge in childhood'. Cognitive constructivism is based on the work of the Swiss biologist and naturalist Jean Piaget. Whilst working with the French psychologist Alfred Binet (the inventor of the first intelligence test), Piaget became curious about the structure of the child's mind. From an analysis of interviews with children of differing ages as they solved problems and his observations of the process, Piaget concluded that older children think in a very different way from younger children. It wasn't simply that older children knew more but that their thought processes had undergone some form of maturational (age-related) change. Piaget continued to study child development for several decades before positing the theory that intellectual development occurs in four distinct stages. Each of these stages is described in detail in this chapter with their advantages and shortcomings discussed.

Chapter 5 extends the concepts introduced in Chapter 4. Vygotsky, a Russian developmental psychologist, developed many of the concepts outlined by Piaget to incorporate the child's social environment. He stressed the fundamental role of social interaction in the development of cognition. Vygotsky believed that each child is born with a basic set of unlearned cognitive functions such as memory and attention that facilitate high-level learning. Since from their earliest moments children are absorbing the rules and mores of their culture, Vygotsky believed that learning can precede understanding; whereas Piaget believed that development precedes learning. According to Vygotsky (1978, p. 57):

> Every function in the child's cultural development appears twice: first, on the social level, and later, on the individual level; first, between people (interpsychological) and then inside the child (intrapsychological).

Both Piaget and Vygotsky believed that young children are curious and actively involved in their own learning and in the discovery and development of new understandings/schema. Whereas Vygotsky placed more emphasis on social contributions to the process of development, Piaget emphasized self-initiated discovery. These points will be considered in greater detail in Chapter 6 where the zone of proximal development, role of culture, social factors, language, peers and educators are explored in detail.

Chapter 6 explores the social learning theories of Bandura and Bronfenbrenner. As previously discussed (see Chapter 3 above), Bandura's social learning theory has its roots in behaviourism. Whilst sharing the experimental approaches of his contemporaries, Bandura argued that to exclude thinking from any theory of learning would be like reducing 'Shakespeare's literary masterpieces to his prior instruction in the mechanics of writing' (Bandura, 1978, p. 350). Social learning theory advocates that individuals, especially children, imitate or copy modelled behaviour from personally observing others, the environment and the mass media. Reflecting the central tenets of traditional behaviourism, Bandura believed that behaviour can be shaped and maintained by reinforcement. He extended this theory to include two aspects of indirect reinforcement termed vicarious and self reinforcement. Vicarious reinforcement or observational learning occurs when a child witnesses the effects of an event and stores it in memory. By way of example, pre-school children refused to wear their seatbelts after watching the children's cartoon character Peppa Pig and her brother George sitting in the back seat of a car without seatbelts. Following complaints from parents, the producers rectified the problem (BBC News, 2010). This example serves to indicate that, consistent with Bandura's theory, the relationship between viewers and television is reciprocal, with each reacting and shaping the other.

Similar themes inform Bronfenbrenner's ecological model of child development. Bronfenbrenner acknowledged the role of media, technology, culture and society on childhood development. Like Bandura, Bronfenbrenner believed that technology has the potential to change and even damage society (Henderson, 1995), and that the child influences and is influenced by their environment. Bronfenbrenner was one of the first psychologists to adopt a holistic perspective on human development. His ecological model of development comprises five interrelated systems each containing the roles, norms and rules that powerfully shape development. Bronfenbrenner recognized that not only is it necessary to understand how the family or school influences human development, but broader influences as well.

Chapter 7 considers Bruner's (1915–present) discovery learning theory of constructivism. Bruner was influenced by Piaget's ideas about cognitive development in children. During the 1940s, his early work focused on the impact of needs, motivations, expectations (mental sets) and their influence on perception. Like Piaget, he emphasizes action and problem solving in children's learning, but like Vygotsky he underlines the role of social interaction, language and instruction in the development of thinking. To achieve this goal, he devised the concept of scaffolding. Whilst the term scaffolding is most closely associated with Bruner, it was coined by Wood, Bruner and Ross (1976) to describe the type of support children need to achieve the zone of development. Though a psychologist by training, Bruner became a prominent figure in education and wrote several influential and highly regarded texts for teachers including *The Process of Education (1960), Toward a Theory of Instruction (1966), The Relevance of Education (1971)* and *The Culture of Education (1996)*. The final section of this chapter includes a detailed review of constructivist and social constructivist theories drawing out similar and disparate threads.

Chapter 8 examines children's learning through the lens of a newly evolving paradigm variously referred to as the new social studies of childhood and the new sociology of childhood. The origins of this theory can be traced to the United Nations Convention on the Rights of the Child (UNCRC, 1989), which was ratified in the UK in 1999. The UNCRC established children's rights to provision, protection and participation and changed the way children were viewed by many social and developmental researchers (Corosa, 2004). In challenging the objectification of children, the UNCRC heralded a well-documented shift away from research being conducted 'on' to research being conducted 'with' children (Porter and Lacey, 2005). Critical of traditional approaches to research on children's learning, proponents of the social studies of childhood reject the empirical methods favoured by behaviourists and critique Piaget's explanation of universal age-related competencies. Advocates of this newly evolving paradigm share the natural methods of enquiry favoured by Piaget and embrace key concepts of the socio-constructivist and ecological theories. This chapter seeks to explore this contemporary theory with reference to more traditional approaches to children's development and learning.

The final chapter of this book offers a departure from theory (Chapter 9). It is written especially for people who work with or care for young children and who would like to enhance children's learning. Consideration is given to the challenges inherent in creating a learning–teaching environment where children play together in creative, investigative and problem-solving ways, where they take ownership of and responsibility for their own learning, and where emotional and imaginative needs are met (Broadbent, 2006, p. 192). In addition, the role of the adult as a facilitator of learning is explored with reference to the theories of Vygotsky, Bronfenbrenner and Bruner. Practical examples from practice pepper and inform this chapter which seeks to demonstrate the dynamic relationship between theory and practice.

Exercise

Before reading further, consider which theorist best explains how children's learning develops. As you read each of the following chapters, we would ask you to continually review your decision and to consider whether the information provided has changed or strengthened your initial view.

RECOMMENDED READING

Fabian, H. & Mould, C. (eds) (2009). *Development and Learning for Very Young Children*. London: Sage.

A useful resource, this book concentrates on children in the 0–3 age range. Fabian and Mould cover a breadth of material, including the stages of child development, development and learning, and policy and practice.

Robson, S. (2009). *Developing, Thinking and Understanding in Young Children*. London and New York: Routledge.

This interesting and challenging text offers an in-depth study of children's thinking and learning. The developing brain and language and communication are discussed through the lens of thinking and learning. Limited to cognitive theory, it offers students an insight into the developing child.

REFERENCES

Bandura, A. (1978). Perceived effectiveness: an explanatory mechanism of behavioral change. In G. Lindzey, C.S. Hall & R.F. Thompson (eds) *Psychology*. New York: Worth.

BBC News (2010). Peppa Pig in seatbelt safety row. Available at: http://news.bbc.co.uk/1/hi/8460753.stm

Broadbent, P. (2006). Developing an understanding of young children's learning through play: the place of observation, interaction and reflection. *British Journal of Educational Research, 32, 2,* 191–207.

Bruner, J.S. (1960). *The Process of Education.* Cambridge, MA: Harvard University Press.

Bruner, J.S. (1966). *Toward a Theory of Instruction.* Cambridge, MA: Belknapp Press.

Bruner, J.S. (1971). *The Relevance of Education.* New York: Norton.

Bruner, J.S. (1996). *The Culture of Education.* Cambridge, MA: Harvard University Press.

Corosa, W.A. (2004). *The Sociology of Childhood (Sociology for a New Century Series),* 2nd edn. Thousand Oaks, CA: Pine Forge Press.

David, T., Goouch, K. & Powell, S. (2011). Play and prescription: the influence of national developments in England. In M. Kernan & E. Singer (eds) *Peer Relationships in Early Childhood Education and Care.* London: Routledge. pp. 49–60.

Dorin, H., Demmin, P.E. & Gabel, D. (1990). *Chemistry: The Study of Matter,* 3rd edn. Englewood Cliffs, NJ: Prentice Hall.

Gardner, H. (1983). *Frames of Mind: The Theory of Multiple Intelligences.* New York: Basic Books.

Henderson, Z.P. (1995). Renewing our social fabric. *Human Ecology, 23, 1,* 16–19.

Hepper, P.G. (1996). Fetal memory: does it exist? What does it do? *ACTA Paediatrica Supplement, 416,* 16–20.

Maslow, A.H. (1943). A theory of human motivation. *Psychological Review, 50, 4, 370–96.*

Porter, J. & Lacey, P. (2005). *Researching Learning Difficulties: A Guide for Practitioners.* London: Paul Chapman Publishing.

United Nations Convention on the Rights of the Child (UNCRC) (1989). Available at: www.unicef.org/crc/

Vygotsky, L.S. (1978). *Mind and Society: The Development of Higher Mental Processes.* Cambridge, MA: Harvard University Press.

Wood, D., Bruner, J.S. & Ross, G. (1976). The role of tutoring in problem solving. *Journal of Child Psychology and Psychiatry, 17, 2,* 81–100.

Woollard, J. (2010). *Psychology for the Classroom: Behaviourism.* Oxon: Routledge.

2

THE FOUNDING FATHERS AND PHILOSOPHIES OF LEARNING

This chapter aims to:

- explore the work of key philosophers and theorists who have influenced thinking and practice in the field of early years education and practice
- examine the work of these philosophers and theorists within the social and historical contexts within which they developed their ideas.

INTRODUCTION

Our understanding of how children think and experience the worlds in which they live is limited. How, for example, do we begin to understand the thoughts expressed by the philosopher Jean-Paul Sartre who lost his father when he was still only a very young child:

> Jean-Baptiste's death was the great event of my life: it returned my mother to her chains and it gave me my freedom … Dying is not everything: you have to die in time. Later on, I felt guilty; a sensitive orphan blames himself: his parents, offended by the sight of him, have retired to their flats in the sky. But I was delighted: my unhappy condition imposed respect and established my importance; I numbered my mourning among my virtues. (Sartre, 1967, p. 15)

How can a child be 'delighted' following his father's death, how can bereavement 'impose respect' and how can mourning be considered a virtue? Why, over time, did Jean-Paul's feelings and emotions turn from feelings of freedom and self-importance to feelings of guilt?

How we view childhood and the manner in which young children are best educated and supported in their development, will change radically in the next few decades. Much of our current thinking is informed by what has been written in the past and is shaped daily by the ever-shifting world in which we live (Zwozdiak-Myers, 2007). Indeed, it has been suggested that it is only in the last 50 years or so that we have really begun to properly understand childhood and child development in any meaningful and measured way (Corsaro, 2005). There is still so much that we do not know and so much we still need to learn. For this reason, it is essential that all of us who work with children, and who study their development, maintain a strong sense of critical reflection and openness in how we view child development and education as well as our own professional practice. Whilst we are guided by the thinking and the theories of those notable individuals who have written about children over the centuries, we are also influenced by the events which structure our own lives and perceptions.

Much of what we do, think and practise has its roots in the work of these philosophers and thinkers who, in many ways, have altered the course of education and learning not only in the UK but across the globe. Indeed, it is largely because of their ideas and their own unique developed practice that we now work with children in the way we do. In order to properly understand these key figures and their views, however, it is important to say something of the events that shaped their own lives, in particular their early lives and the world they were born into.

John Locke (1632–1704)

John Locke is considered by many to be one of England's most enlightened thinkers. Locke was born into a world where 'wife beating' was considered to be the legal right of a husband, where a woman's entire belongings became the property of her husband following marriage, and where women and children were expected by society to be unwavering in their obedience to their husbands and fathers. King Charles I was still relatively new to the throne of England having begun his rule as monarch in 1629. In fact, John Locke was to live through the beheading of King Charles, the Civil War in England, Cromwell's Protectorate from 1654 to 1658, the Restoration of King Charles II in 1659, the reigns of King James II, and then William and Mary and, finally, the reign of Queen Anne.

Locke published *Some Thoughts Concerning Education* in 1693, in which he set out his philosophy of education. His views on education were radical for the time and though he wrote about these nearly 400 years ago, they continue to influence the way we think about the education and rearing of children today. Locke was a truly influential thinker and he belongs to that group of English philosophers known as the *empiricists* who believed that our knowledge and understanding of the world comes about through 'sensory experience'.

This view lies very much at the heart of what we now know as the 'sciences', at the root of which lies the concept of 'empirical thinking' whereby we observe, acquire and quantify data. Closely linked to this view was Locke's strongly held belief that individuals should use their own reason to explore what is true and what is not, as opposed to simply accepting what they are told by those in authority. He further rejected the place of superstition in the thinking of individuals.

Locke held the view that when individuals are born they begin life as a 'blank slate' (often referred to as *tabula rasa*) upon which is written their life experiences gained through the senses. This was, Locke believed, the very essence of learning and the basis for the acquisition of knowledge. In more recent years, particularly during the post-war years, this empirical view that we could understand experience through the observation and measurement of behaviours, which are in response to external sensory stimuli, grew in strength, especially within the field of psychology, and came to underpin that branch of psychology known as the behaviourist tradition. Not only did this philosophy of empiricism offer a theory, it also offered psychology a methodology, at the core of which was the observation and recording of behaviours (Gross, 1992; Smith et al., 2003). This is quite different from the nativist view, which saw individuals as inheriting abilities. Here, we can see quite clearly the link between philosophy and theory.

Exercise

What benefits can early years practitioners gain from observing and recording the behaviours of young children and how reliable can their interpretations of these observations be?

Locke saw the purpose of education as that of instilling within individuals a strong sense of virtue: 'I place virtue as the first and most necessary of those endowments that belong to a man or a gentleman' (2001, p. 148). Locke also placed great emphasis upon the importance of learning how to learn. Here, it is possible to see just how far ahead of his time he was, as in recent decades the emphasis that has been placed upon learning how to learn and upon learning styles has grown dramatically. In addition to this emphasis upon employing thinking in a different and more structural manner, Locke also placed considerable emphasis upon the importance of language and communication, and perhaps most interestingly, given the nature of society at the time, the idea that learning should be enjoyable. In many respects, we can argue that John Locke laid down the building blocks for future thinking around the importance of play and the development of language. In doing so, he prepared the way for others to address the importance of education and learning in young children.

Jean-Jacques Rousseau (1712–1778)

Born in Geneva in 1712, it is worth considering that perhaps one of the most defining moments of Jean-Jacques Rousseau's life was the death of his mother some nine days after giving birth to him. This must have had a great influence upon Rousseau and upon his views regarding early childhood and parenting. Later, at the age of 10, Rousseau's father moved away and left Jean-Jacques to be reared by relatives. Shortly after leaving, his father remarried and the young Rousseau saw very little of him from that time on. This was clearly a second major loss experienced by the young Rousseau. Such events in the life of any young child will be central to the way in which they go about constructing the world in which they live. It can be suggested that much of Rousseau's childhood would have been unhappy due to the death of his mother and the subsequent loss of his father. It should also be recognized that Rousseau was born into a world where the French revolution had not yet taken place and it was less than 50 years earlier, in 1665, that the Great Plague had hit London, leaving behind it such incredible devastation and grief.

At the very core of Rousseau's philosophy of education is the view that all human beings are born 'good'. Rousseau believed, as many of his time did, that individuals inherit much of what would contribute to their potential make-up. Whilst he held the view that individuals inherit the propensity to be good, he also saw the societies within which individuals grow up as being agents of potential perversion. Such a view can still be found today, with individuals in some quarters emphasizing the adverse impact on children of such factors as elements of the media, materialism and an exaggerated notion of rights without responsibilities. Rousseau chose to develop his ideas about life and education through the publication of his book *Emile*, in which he introduced the reader to the character of a young boy. In the book, Emile begins to be introduced to lessons in morality whilst in infanthood. These lessons are then extended through adolescence and into adulthood whilst all the time being overseen by a tutor who, Rousseau proposed, crucially offers direction and guidance.

Rousseau saw education as the means by which the natural make-up of individuals could be developed to not only improve them but also to improve society through the manner in which individuals engage with one another. For Rousseau, the importance of developing the character of individuals was a fundamental goal of those education processes that took place in schools. This should not, he felt, be overshadowed by an emphasis upon the giving and receiving of information as characterized by so many schools at the time. Here, we can draw similarities with the recent emphasis that governments in the UK have placed upon citizenship, and the expectations made upon early years practitioners and teachers to develop positive values within the children they manage.

For Rousseau, the role of tutor was of the upmost importance and required the shaping of those environments within which the young person is introduced to learning. In this way, Rousseau suggested that growing children acquire increased awareness of the world around them, but more particularly, they increase their understanding of such essentials as humility, honesty and dishonesty, and respect for themselves and for others. Rousseau saw the primary function of education as being 'l'art de former des homes' or the art of forming men. Interestingly, Rousseau saw the role of the tutor as being that of guiding the child in such a way that the child learns the difference between right and wrong, not as a result of being punished, as was common at the time, but as a result of understanding the consequences of their actions. Here, again, we can see strong similarities with the thinking of modern educationalists in the UK who, in the 1970s and 1980s argued for the banning of all physical punishment in schools and the promotion amongst growing children of self-awareness and the feelings of others. Such a view is the norm now in all pre-school, primary and post-primary education. At the time that Rousseau lived, however, it was very much not the case. Indeed, it was generally accepted by those living at that time that all individuals, though essentially 'good', were in fact born into the world with impulses, drives and needs, which lay beneath their 'goodness' and which could, if not harnessed, lead to, amongst other things, 'wickedness'. Rousseau, therefore, saw a primary function of the tutor, or teacher, as being that of channelling these impulses and drives, and giving some form of positive expression to them.

Rousseau is recognized as being one of the first proponents of developmental education. Indeed, he considered that individuals progress through a number of stages, the first being that of birth to around 12 years of age. It was during this stage, Rousseau believed, that the child was influenced and directed in their thinking and actions, and by their emotions and impulses. The next stage takes the child to 16 when, Rousseau considered, reason begins to take over from emotions. After the age of 16, the child moves through to adulthood.

Rousseau's views can be considered as revolutionary for the time and we see his notion of stages being echoed in the work of more recent theorists such as Jean Piaget and Eric Erikson. Rousseau's philosophies have also much in common with, amongst others, those of Maria Montessori and John Dewey who will be referred to later. It is useful at this point to now turn to the work of one further key figure who was born towards the end of Rousseau's life and whose influence upon the way we work with young children has lasted for over 150 years, and is even currently experiencing something of a revival (Miller and Pound, 2011, p. 64).

Friedrich Froebel (1782–1852)

Froebel was born in 1782 in Oberweißach in what is now Germany, and experienced the death of his mother some nine months after his birth. This loss affected him deeply and must certainly have had an impact on the way he perceived childhood. In the years following his birth, he received little comfort and it was not until 1792 when he was some 10 years of age that he experienced a more caring environment when he went to live with an uncle who was a caring and affectionate man. In 1818, he married Wilhelmine who then died in 1839 leaving no children. Friedrich remarried Louise some years later in 1851. As a young man, Froebel was impulsive and after trying a number of jobs he joined a school in Frankfurt as a teacher under the direction of Anton Gruner who had organized his school along the principles set out by Johann Pestalozzi, a Swiss educator and reformer who advocated progressive methods in teaching. It was whilst working at this school that Froebel realized his desire to be a teacher, and in 1816 he opened his own school. In 1826, he published *On the Education of Man*, which set out his philosophy and the methods he had used in his own school. In 1831, he was invited by the Swiss government to become involved in the training of teachers working with young children. Later, in 1837, he opened a school for very young children, which he renamed, after some time, '*kindergarten*'.

Froebel was one of the most influential thinkers of his time and his philosophy of education continues to influence practice today. Froebel viewed play as central to the education of children and their future development and though most, if not all, practitioners working with young children today would see this as a given, it was not always the case. Froebel believed passionately in the importance of children expressing themselves through their own individual play as well as through play with others. This view, however, stood in marked contrast to much of the practice of the time when many young children found themselves in schools being unhappily 'drilled' and regularly 'chastised' by teachers. Froebel, it can be suggested, liberated the notion of play and made it central to the education of young children. Some 30 years ago, Tizard and Hughes commented as follows:

> The value of learning through play was first put forward by the German educationalist Friedrich Froebel … The kindergarten and nursery school movement which developed from his writings freed young children from the tyranny of sitting in rows chanting and writing ABC. (1984, p. 4)

Now consider, for example, the opening lines of Charles Dickens's novel *Hard Times*, first published in 1854, two years after Froebel's death, where the fictional headmaster of a school in the north of England is setting out his own philosophy of education:

> Now, what I want is, Facts. Teach these boys and girls nothing but Facts. Facts alone are wanted in life. Plant nothing else, and root out everything else. You can only form the minds of reasoning animals upon Facts: nothing else will ever be of service to them. This is the principle on which I bring up my own children, and this is the principle on which I bring up these children. Stick to Facts, Sir! (p. 1)

Though the headmaster and school were fictional, Dickens was, nevertheless, attempting to draw to public attention, and to policy and decision makers, the scandalous nature of much of the teaching and learning that took place in schools at this time. Years later, the renowned academic, philosopher and theologian C.S. Lewis (author of the *Chronicles of Narnia*) was also able to speak in less than positive terms about how dreadful aspects of his own early education were. Lewis's biographer A.N. Wilson has since written as follows:

> C.S. Lewis remained obsessed by Wynyard (Lewis' preparatory school) for the rest of his life. Although he spent only eighteen months as a pupil there, he devoted nearly a tenth of his autobiography to describing it, in the most lurid terms, as a 'concentration camp'. (1991, p. 23)

Unlike many educators and thinkers of his time, Froebel held the view that individuals were born creative and, through their industry and active belief in God, developed as good members of society. In this way, he argued, they came to better understand the world in which they lived. It was because of his belief in the importance of play that Froebel set about creating specialized educational *materials* to be used by children in their early education. Indeed, one of the many legacies left by Froebel to educators were these *materials* or *gifts* as he, himself, called them. These *gifts* included, for example, shapes such as spheres and blocks and were purposefully used to assist in the process of stimulating the thinking and learning of young children (it is possible to view some of these *gifts* in the Froebel College at Roehampton University). Froebel believed that being active was very important for children. He referred to the activities he developed for children as *occupations*. Froebel also recognized and understood the value of music in the education of young children and the value of singing to accompany play. His beliefs are now taken as accepted by many practitioners working with young children.

John Dewey (1859–1952)

What is remarkable about John Dewey is the span of history through which he lived. Born in America some two years before the outbreak of the American Civil War and in the same year as the infamous American outlaw Billy the Kid and the French artist Seurat, and the first publication of Charles Dickens's novel, *A Tale of Two Cities*, he ended his life seven years after the end of the Second World War and just eight years before the 'swinging sixties' exploded with the music of Elvis Presley, the Beatles and Bob Dylan. Dewey was born into a world where Queen Victoria ruled the British Empire, where British veterans were coming to terms with their recent experiences of war in the Crimea and the Charge of the Light Brigade, and the British nation was applauding the work of Florence Nightingale. In a sense, he bridged the gap between the old and the modern. Dewey grew up and lived in an America where there were extreme racial tensions in parts of the country and where children in some states were not accorded the same civil and human rights as others, because of their colour.

It is important to consider the work of John Dewey in greater depth because of the controversial nature of his ideas and because of the significant influence he has had on educational practice in the past 50 years, and which continues even today. Perhaps a good starting point for considering the influence that John Dewey has had on the education system can be found in the words of the American philosopher Nell Noddings (2005), cited in Pring:

> not only has he (*Dewey*) been hailed as the savior of American education by those who welcome greater involvement of students in their own planning and activity [but also] he has been called 'worse than Hitler' by some who felt that he infected schools with epistemological and moral relativism and substituted socialization for true education. (2007, p. 3)

Pring also cites, as part of his own experience in relation to the influence of Dewey, the following incident:

> Indeed, when I came to Oxford in 1989, I was seated at dinner next to Lord Keith Joseph, who had been Secretary of State for Education under Prime Minister Margaret Thatcher. He accused me of being responsible for all the problems in our schools – because I had introduced teachers to John Dewey. (2007, p. 3)

It must be recognized at the outset that Dewey was writing at a time when much of the learning and teaching that took place in schools was of a very formal nature. Pre-school education was ill-understood and much of early years practice that we now take for granted simply did not exist. It should also be remembered that as Dewey was growing up, and reflecting upon his own experiences of education and how children could be educated, that society across the emerging industrialized world was so extraordinarily varied. In contrast to the experiences of his early life in the USA, there persisted across the Atlantic in Victorian England, for example, an infamous practice known as *baby farming*.

Due to their being no reliable means of contraception at the time, many young women in Victorian England, often from 'good' families, found themselves giving birth to children outside of wedlock. Such births resulted most frequently in a great deal of social stigma. Any form of abortion, which at the time was illegal, had its dangers and all too frequently resulted in death. Mothers or fathers who abandoned their offspring at this time were also subject to severe punishment by the law. Because of the harsh penalties meted out by Victorian courts, many of these mothers 'farmed' out their young children to other families for what was then a sizeable sum of money, usually around £10–20. There were no regular adoption services during this period and the practice of 'farming' out children became widely practised. Some of the women who took on these children were quite unscrupulous and many of these children became lost to their parents. Amongst these 'baby farmers' were some women who maltreated the children placed in their care with some even murdering them and a small number being identified as serial killers. 'baby farmers' who were caught murdering their children faced the death penalty and were hanged. One such case was that of Selina Wedge who was hanged on 15 August 1878 at Bodmin in the county of Cornwall following the murder of her illegitimate son. At the time of Selina Wedge's execution, Dewey would have been around 19 years of age, Montessori about 8 years of age, and Steiner about 17 years of age.

DEWEY AND EDUCATION

Dewey has become associated in the minds of many with the notion of *child-centered education*. At the heart of Dewey's philosophy of education lies the importance of understanding children's experiences. It should be noted, however, that a common misunderstanding of Dewey's philosophy is that he supported free, student-led education. In fact, he believed strongly that the education of children required clear structure. Dewey also believed that children needed support and direction in structuring their own learning in order to gain the maximum benefit. Like many philosophers and theorists before and after him, Dewey was an exponent of the view that educators must acknowledge the uniqueness of each individual child. This uniqueness, Dewey believed, was formed genetically as well as experientially. Arguably, Dewey was ahead of his time in that he believed that each child engaged with the curriculum offered by their schools in qualitatively different ways. Because of this, he argued that the curriculum should take account of and allow for these differences. Dewey was also an exponent of the view that education should be seen as having a wider social purpose, that of preparing children to become effective members of their society and to be valued by their societies. Indeed, Dewey saw education and democracy as being intrinsically linked.

> **Exercise**
>
> To what extent should early years practitioners engage in preparing young children to be 'good' citizens in the future and to what extent should they be expected to 'teach' behaviour?

Central to Dewey's philosophy of education were his views drawn from his *Laboratory School* where he could subject his ideas and theoretical position to scrutiny and analysis (Dewey started Laboratory Schools in 1896 in Chicago, with children being admitted from nursery to the 12th grade). Pring offers the following:

> behind Dewey's experimental school was a particular view of the normal young learner: someone who is curious and interested, but whose curiosity and interests had been sapped by modes of learning which took no account of that *interest* in learning. (2007, p. 16)

Dewey espoused two important notions. First, schools should be seen as communities in themselves, and second, educators cannot alter the past experiences of children. This also applies to those working in early years settings. Dewey argued that educators must deal with the present and the future. By engaging in the process of understanding the past experiences of their pupils, they can, however, be more informed and more cognizant of how to effect change over what the pupil will learn and in what way it is directly relevant to each pupil. Pring offers a summary of Dewey's views:

> First, the school should be an extension of the home and the community ... Second ..., the school should value manual and practical activity ... Third, the interests of young people were to be treated as of importance in their own right, not simply as something that can be harnessed to the aims of the teacher for the purpose of motivating them to do things that they are not really interested in ... Fourth ... their (*school subjects*) value lies in their usefulness ... Fifth, a young person whose interests are taken seriously and whose teacher seeks to develop those interests ... will be disciplined by the pursuit of those interests – making the regime of externally imposed discipline irrelevant. (2007, pp. 15–17)

Taking Dewey's views into account then it can be argued that we all learn from what we do. In the case of young children their experiences are of great immediate value in that they will affect future experiences and learning. For Dewey, however, experiences have no attached value in themselves. Rather, it is what each individual draws from the experience that is important, and no two individuals will encounter an experience in exactly the same way. What will be beneficial for one person might be devastating for another. We now turn to a figure who has, some would argue, dominated a great deal of our thinking and practice in the area of early years.

Maria Montessori (1870–1952)

Maria Montessori is a name that has universal meaning and she is recognized as being a hugely creative and influential figure in the world of early years education. Born in 1870 in Italy, she was the first of her gender to become a medical doctor. Maria was also a single parent and, during childhood, chose to attend a single-sex school for boys at the age of 13 as a means of educating herself to take up a career as an engineer. Maria was deeply interested in the needs of children with learning difficulties, what we now refer to as 'Special Educational Needs'. Maria had considerable success with these children who at the time were considered uneducable. She was appointed Director of the *Scuola Ortofrenica*, which was one of a number of institutions in Italy which looked after those with mental health problems.

Montessori viewed the course of development in young children as being guided by directives that are already located within the child's nature (Feez, 2010). The Montessori teacher, therefore, places great emphasis upon the environment in which the child learns. In a sense, the teacher becomes the guardian of that environment and, by altering it, the teacher enables the child to develop at their natural pace, thus allowing their creativity to flourish and their learning to be supported.

Montessori introduced the notion of the *Casa dei Bambini* or *Children's House,* in which the teacher created an environment that offered stimulation and where children were free to develop their learning in a natural and individualized way. Montessori strongly advocated the importance of young children learning through their senses. She also considered it fundamental to the education process that children should take responsibility for their own learning. To assist them in this, Montessori took the initiative of designing the furniture within her *Children's House* so that it was of a suitable size for the children, a factor we nowadays take for granted.

At the heart of the Montessori Method lies the notion of 'Planes', or Stages, that children pass through on their learning journey. It is during the first 'Plane' that the child experiences significant levels of change in the areas of physical, social and emotional development. Here, the infant starts to take their first steps, use their first words and engage with others. By the time they are ready to move to the next Plane, they can run, jump and climb, and engage in conversation with others using complex and sophisticated language structures and vocabulary. They are beginning to understand the feelings of others and adapt their own behaviours and actions in accordance with these. In addition, they are learning to interact with those around them, make friendships and adapt to the complexities of social interaction outside of their families. It is during this first Plane that children also develop their abilities in such important areas as memory, information processing, and expressive and receptive language, and it is during this Plane that adults working with young children typically observe the greatest steps in learning taking place. Within the first Plane, Montessori identified what she termed 11 'sensitive' periods: Movement; Language; Small Objects; Order; Music; Grace and Courtesy; Refinement of the Senses; Writing Fascination; Reading; Spatial Relationships; and Mathematics. These will be discussed more fully in Chapter 9.

One interesting element of Montessori's original thinking, however, is her lack of enthusiasm for pretend and imaginative play, which, given her emphasis upon child-centred education and early development, may appear surprising. In fact, Montessori saw limited value in this type of play, preferring, instead, to place greater emphasis upon the value of practical activities: 'She preferred to encourage children actually to serve meals, for example, and to clear up around the house themselves, rather than play at mealtimes in a "play house"' (Smith et al., 2003, p. 230).

Exercise

At the heart of the Montessori Method lies the notion of 'Planes', or Stages. How useful is it to think of children's development in terms of Stages?

Having looked at key elements underpinning the ideas of Maria Montessori, we now turn to those of Rudolf Steiner who, like Montessori, has left an enormous legacy, which continues to guide the thinking and practice of many practitioners working with young children today.

Rudolf Steiner (1861–1925)

Rudolf Steiner was born in what is now part of Croatia and was then part of the Austro-Hungarian Empire. He was born in February 1861, two years after the birth of John Dewey, and died in 1925. Steiner was accomplished in many areas; he was a very competent linguist, mathematician, architect, scientist and classical scholar. Throughout his life, Steiner remained true to his convictions that a fundamental aim of education was to develop the potential of children. It is clear that Steiner's philosophy and his activities and efforts in the field of education have had a major impact upon practitioners, writers and academics today.

There are currently over 1000 Steiner schools and over 2000 early years establishments across the world. Though the original philosophy remains constant, many Steiner schools throughout the world have evolved in different ways, which, in itself, reflects the highly creative and scholarly approach originally adopted by Steiner himself. Steiner founded his first school in the city of Stuttgart following an invitation to do so from a leading industrialist, Waldorf Astoria, who was the owner of a large cigarette factory. The purpose of opening the school was to educate the children of those who worked in the factory, hence the legacy by which some Steiner schools are still referred to as *Steiner Waldorf* schools. This school was built upon progressive views of education and was a huge success. Steiner involved himself in all aspects of the organization of this school and even engaged in the training of the teachers.

Steiner believed that the function of education was to respond to the changing needs of children, and not only their physical needs but, more importantly, their cognitive and emotional needs (Goddard Blythe, 2008, cited in Miller and Pound, 2011). Steiner schools do not have a head teacher and teachers share the responsibilities.

Key points that underpin the Steiner philosophy are as follows. In the first years of a child's education and up to age 7, there is significant emphasis placed upon play, art and drawing, upon the natural world of the child, and upon links between art and science. Prior to age 7, children are not formally taught to read, the idea being that children will learn to read more effectively if they have developed emotionally and socially. Children are introduced to reading and writing as well as mathematics later than children in other schools. The belief is that children, when older, will be more mature and will acquire formal literacy and numeracy more easily and with less potential stress. Interestingly, the Steiner philosophy holds that children should be taught to write before being taught to read. Once again, it is worth drawing comparisons between this philosophy and current practice in the UK, which advocates the learning of phonics by children when they first enter school at around the age of 5.

Children are encouraged to sing each day and to learn to play musical instruments. They are also introduced to the idea of making their own lesson books, which they write and illustrate. Assessment of children is carried out mainly through observation by the teacher who focuses upon emotional and social aspects as well as academic progress. The child, where possible, keeps the same teacher until the secondary stage, thereby building upon the importance of relationships and the teacher's knowledge of the child's emotional and social development.

Teachers working in Steiner settings use a 'narrative' approach to learning, which places particular emphasis upon listening and involves young children in the internal representation of characters and the development of imagination. Having been introduced to material in the form of a story on a given day, for example, the children are required to revisit the content on the following day and retell it, the aim being to improve spoken language and memory. When these processes of listening and recalling are worked through, the children can then write these down. Again, it is worth considering how valuable this process can be in our modern society when many children come to school with poor listening skills, delayed language and poor vocabulary (Palmer, 2006; Zwozdiak-Myers, 2007).

In part, Steiner's emphasis upon the individuality of education came about because of his own extensive work with individual children. It is interesting to make comparisons with current practice in the majority of developed countries whereby the needs of individual children, especially those with learning difficulties, have become central to many teaching programmes and practice. It is also interesting to make comparisons with the nature of the curricula currently offered in state schools in the UK and the degree of emphasis or not that is placed upon creativity and independent learning.

Rachel McMillan (1859–1917) and Margaret McMillan (1860–1931)

Rachel McMillan was born on 25 March 1859 in New York, USA. Her sister Margaret was born on 20 July 1860. Rachel and Margaret's parents had emigrated from Scotland some years before in 1840. Sadly, their father James died, along with their sister Elizabeth, in 1865 when Margaret was aged just 5. Their mother then returned to Scotland taking her two daughters with her. Some years later in 1877, their mother also died leaving the two girls without any parents; Margaret was only 17. Following the death of their grandmother in 1888, Rachel moved to London to be closer to Margaret. Much of London at this time was characterized by poverty, poor sanitation and a need for social reform. In fact, it was during the year that Rachel moved to London that the infamous murderer Jack the Ripper became linked to five murders. It was in 1899 that school attendance became compulsory and it was into this London that both sisters threw themselves with zeal, enthusiasm and a strong vision of how young children should be educated.

Following a sustained campaign, the McMillan sisters achieved the successful introduction of free school meals for children, following the passing of the Provision of School Meals Act in 1906. The two sisters were also responsible for introducing regular medical inspections of school-aged children with the first clinic being opened in 1908. It must be remembered that at this time there was exceptional poverty in England, and especially in the cities. London at this time contained many slum areas where infant mortality was extremely high and the standard of living extremely low. In 1841, for example, Londoners could, on average, expect to live until the age of 35. Seventy years later, in 1911, they could, on average, expect to live until they were 50 (Hall, 1998, p. 695). Many houses had little sanitation and families were crowded into tiny areas within houses, often sharing only single rooms. Most individuals of the time who died did so because of infectious diseases, with many very young babies dying due to diarrhoea caused by disease-carrying flies. It is estimated (Horn, 1997) that in the first half of the nineteenth century, around 30,000 homeless children frequented the streets of London, often impoverished, undernourished and sleeping rough. In the previous decades, between 1831 and 1866, some 140,000 individuals died from cholera.

Like Montessori, and others, the McMillan sisters believed that the first years of a child's life were extremely important for future development. In fact, they founded what is now known as the *Nursery School Movement*. In many respects, they can be viewed as social reformers. They also placed great emphasis upon the importance of open-air learning, which could be seen as a precursor to the current emphasis placed by many early years practitioners upon playing out doors and, more recently, 'Forest Schools'. It should be remembered, however, that when the McMillan sisters encouraged outdoor learning, they were working largely with children from very poor and disadvantaged backgrounds. Nowadays, it is considered wholly appropriate for children to play outside. In fact, playing outside is viewed by most early years practitioners to be an important part of the child's curriculum. In past decades, however, this was not always the case as playing outside was often seen as merely a 'break' from within-class activities.

In 1904, Margaret published *Education through the Imagination*, in which she argued against the commonly held notion of the time that imagination was of little use to children in their learning. She argued, in fact, that imagination was very important and should be a key element in the education of children and their learning. Moreover, she considered it to be an important element for the betterment of society. This is, of course, a view widely held by many today. The McMillan sisters also involved the young children in their nurseries in caring for animals and plants as a way of instilling within them the values of caring for themselves and for others. Margaret was influential in the training of teachers and, some years after the death of her sister, she founded the Rachel McMillan College in 1930 because she strongly believed in the importance of proper training for those working in nurseries.

Summary

This chapter has examined a range of philosophies that have influenced the way in which we view young children and their social, emotional and cognitive abilities and potential. Particular consideration was given to the historical context within which each philosophy was founded and the nature of society at the time. Whilst not all philosophers agree with each other, they, nevertheless, all offer insights into how we think about children and their development. They set the scene for us to explore and to question ourselves and others about what are effective and meaningful ways of working with young children. This is now more important than ever as the world in which we live is changing more quickly than ever before.

RECOMMENDED READING

Feez, S. (2010). *Montessori and Early Childhood*. London: Sage.

A detailed and readable text, which offers a comprehensive account of Montessori's contribution to our understanding of children's development.

Johnson, J. (2010). *Positive and Trusting Relationships with Children in Early Years Settings*. Exeter: Learning Matters.

A comprehensive, readable and visual text offering the student and practitioner a great deal of relevant knowledge.

REFERENCES

Corsaro, W. (2005). *The Sociology of Childhood*. London: Sage.
Dickens, C. (1854). *Hard Times*. London: Wordsworth.

Feez, S. (2010). *Montessori and Early Childhood*. London: Sage.

Froebel, F. (1826). *On the Education of Man*. Keilhau, Leipzig: Weinbach.

Gross, R. (1992). *Psychology: The Science of Mind and Behaviour*. London: Hodder & Stoughton.

Hall, P. (1998). *Cities in Civilization*. London: Weidenfeld & Nicolson.

Horn, P. (1997). *The Victorian Town Child*. Stroud: Sutton.

Locke, J. (2001). *Some Thoughts Concerning Education*. The Harvard Classics. New York: P.F. Collier & Son, 1909–14; Bartleby.com, 2001 (www.bartleby.com/37/1/). Originally published 1693.

McMillan, M. (1904). *Education through the Imagination*. London: Swann Sonnenschein.

Miller, L. & Pound, L. (2011). *Theories and Approaches to Learning in the Early Years*. London: Sage.

Palmer, S. (2006). *Toxic Childhood*. London: Orion Books.

Pring, R. (2007). *John Dewey: A Philosopher of Education for Our Time?* London: Continuum International Publishing Group.

Rousseau, J.J. (1911). *Emile*. London: J.M. Dent.

Sartre, J.P. (1967). *Words*. Harmondsworth: Penguin.

Smith, K.S., Cowie, H. & Blades, M. (2003). *Understanding Children's Development*, 4th edn. Oxford: Blackwell.

Tizard, B. & Hughes, M. (1984). *Young Children Learning: Talking and Thinking at Home and at School*. London: Fontana Press.

Wilson, A.N. (1991). *C.S. Lewis: A Biography*. London: Flamingo.

Zwozdiak-Myers, P. (ed.) (2007). *Childhood and Youth Studies*. Exeter: Learning Matters.

3 CLASSICAL AND OPERANT CONDITIONING: THE EARLY YEARS EXPERIENCE

This chapter aims to:

- familiarize students with classical and operant conditioning learning theories
- illustrate these theories using practical examples
- highlight similarities and differences between early learning theories.

INTRODUCTION

This chapter explores early attempts by theorists to explain the origins of learning. It begins with the work of Pavlov before exploring the expansion of his theory by Watson, Thorndike and Skinner. Watson applied the principles identified by Pavlov to children and founded a new school of thought termed *behaviourism*. Behavourism is premised on the notion that an association can develop between a stimulus and a response. For example, the fire bell rings (stimulus) and you leave the building (response). These associations are thought to form the basis of learning. According to behaviourism, behaviour can be studied in a systematic and observable manner with no consideration given to how a person experiences, thinks about or perceives their world.

Few early childhood students will be familiar with the term behaviourism and even fewer with the concepts that underpin this theory. Yet most will have some knowledge of programmes such as *Nanny 911*, *Super Nanny*, *Jo Frost*, *The House of Tiny Terrors* and even *It's Me or the Dog*. Each of these programmes is predicated on behaviourist principles. Similarly, most early years settings use star charts and smiley face stickers to shape and maintain appropriate behaviour, and time out or a naughty step or chair to discourage inappropriate behaviour. It is these important early learning theories which form the focus of the present chapter. The chapter includes a number of practical examples, exercises and a comparative table (see Table 3.2 at the end of the Chapter) to highlight similarities and differences in the theories discussed.

IVAN PAVLOV AND CLASSICAL CONDITIONING

Ivan Pavlov (1849–1936)

A Russian physiologist, Pavlov was born on 14 September 1849 in the village of Ryazan. His father was a priest. Pavlov was the oldest of 11 children, six of whom died during childhood. He married and had three sons and a daughter. His life's work focused on identifying the link between digestion and salivation using dogs. His efforts were rewarded when he was awarded the Nobel Prize in Physiology or Medicine (1904) for his work on the underlying mechanisms in the digestive system in mammals. Quite by chance, Pavlov noticed that the dogs salivated when no food was presented. This led him to develop a theory of conditioned reflexes (explained in the body of this chapter). Pavlov's theory, termed classical conditioning, offered the first testable and verifiable account of how some forms of learning take place. His theory has had a major influence on the field of psychology and education.

Pavlov conducted a series of laboratory experiments into the relationship between salivation and digestion in dogs. The research involved cutting the dog's salivary glands and re-attaching them to the outside of the dog's cheek where they were fixed to test tubes. Using this technique, Pavlov was able to accurately measure dog salivation before, during and after digestion. During his experiments, he noticed that the dogs drooled when a laboratory assistant entered the room. Observing the dogs' behaviour over time, Pavlov concluded that the dogs started drooling in the expectation that they would be fed. Even when there was no food brought for the dogs, the mere sight of the laboratory assistants was enough to make the dogs drool. Pavlov termed this 'associated learning', meaning the dogs had built up an association between the laboratory assistant and food. Fascinated by this form of learning, Pavlov found that he could train the dogs to drool to the sound of a bell.

Pavlov described the process in the following way, and by giving each aspect a different term (see Figure 3.1 opposite).

Consider the following examples of learning that appear to have been lost but can quickly be recovered.

1   Your setting has a 'good manners policy'. Each child soon learns to say 'thank you' when you give them their morning break. After the Christmas holiday, you notice that some children have stopped saying 'thank you'. After just one or two reminders, the children say 'thank you' again.

1   When the dog is given food it salivates/drools.

Drooling when food is given was termed an *unconditioned response* (UCR), while the food is an *unconditioned stimulus* (UCS).

2   A bell is presented and rung immediately before food arrives – initially, the dog does not drool. The bell is a *conditioned stimulus* (CS).

3   After a number of pairings of the bell and food, the dog drools in anticipation of food on every hearing of the bell. Pavlov termed this a *conditioned response* (CR).

Even when Pavlov manipulated the bell's ring tone to a higher or lower pitch, the sound made the dog drool. Pavlov called this *generalization*. He also noted that, when a bell is rung without food, the dog's drooling response eventually weakens and seems to disappear. Pavlov termed this reaction *extinction*. Importantly, he noticed that the dog's response had not gone but was *latent* and could be quickly relearnt – he labelled this *spontaneous recovery*. This is an important point and one you will notice in practice.

Figure 3.1   Classical conditioning

2   Josh (aged 6) keeps his bike at his nanny's house where there is a garden. Nanny has been sick in hospital for several months and Josh is excited when they go to visit her at home. Josh goes out to play on his bike but finds he keeps falling off. Frustrated, he tells his mummy that he has forgotten how to ride his bike but she encourages him to try again. She holds the back of the seat for a minute and, after a few wobbles, watches as he rides off by himself.

Pavlov concluded that once learnt, associations are difficult to erase. The notion that learned associations can be dormant but reappear when a trigger is reintroduced has implications for those trying to overcome phobias, drug, alcohol and gambling addictions, or learning healthy eating habits. Although Pavlov's experiments were confined to the laboratory, as we will see in the examples listed and Watson's work with phobias, classical conditioning offers a robust explanation for some forms of learning.

Classical conditioning in action

1   A small child is frightened by a large growling dog. The child cries out in fear. When this child next sees a large dog, they may start to cry. *An association has been made between fear and the dog.* This fear can generalize to all dogs. Over time, the initial cause may be forgotten but the fear remains.

(Cont'd)

(Cont'd)

2 A teacher uses a bell to signal quiet time. When the bell rings, the children fold their arms on their desk and rest their head on their hands. Over time, picking up the bell is sufficient for the children to fold their arms and rest their heads. *An association has been made between the bell and quiet time.*

3 Joel is feeling quite poorly and hasn't eaten for two days. To coax him to eat, his Mum makes his favourite chicken soup. Joel is tempted; he takes a spoonful of soup and is promptly sick. Joel never eats chicken soup again. As an adult, Joel has forgotten this incident but still feels sick at the thought of chicken soup. *An association has been made between the soup and sickness.*

WATSON AND BEHAVIOURISM

John B. Watson (1878–1958)

An American psychologist, Watson was born on 9 January 1878 in North Carolina. After a scandalous divorce, Watson married his student, Jones. Inspired by the work of Pavlov, Watson applied the principles of classical conditioning to children. He founded a new school of thinking – 'behaviourism' – in America in 1913. For more than 50 years, classical conditioning had a major influence on teaching and learning until the late 1960s when it was challenged by Piaget's discovery learning theory.

Impressed by this simple explanation of learning, Watson was the first to extend Pavlov's findings to humans. His seminal work drew heavily on the principles of classical conditioning and informed the development of a new branch of psychology entitled 'behaviourism'. Behaviourist theory is based upon the notion that all behaviour is acquired through conditioning. By today's standards, Watson's laboratory experiments with young children appear cruel and are certainly unethical. By way of example, Watson was interested in discovering whether he could induce a fear reaction in a child who showed no previous fear, and reduce fear in a toddler with a known fear. Watson's experiments are detailed in the case studies below.

The Case of Little Albert (1920)

Although there are varying accounts of the experiments conducted on Little Albert, it is generally agreed that his mother was a wet nurse in a children's hospital. When Albert was approximately 9 months old, Watson and his student Rayner tested the baby's reaction to a range of objects including a white rat, a dog, masks with and without hair, cotton wool and a hammer. They concluded that Albert was a healthy and stolid little boy whose only fear was the noise produced when a steel bar was struck by a hammer creating a loud bang. At approximately 11 months, Albert was introduced to a white rat. To induce fear, Watson crept up behind the baby and hit the bar with the hammer. This process was repeated seven times until the baby cried when shown a white rat. His fear generalized to the extent that Albert cried when shown a range of soft white objects including cotton wool, a Santa Claus mask and Watson's white hair.

Little Albert's mother is reported to have left the hospital before Watson could remove Albert's fears and, until quite recently, little was known about his whereabouts. Beck, Levinson and Irons (2009) spent seven years tracking Little Albert and concluded that Little Albert was a pseudonym used to protect the anonymity of a boy named Douglas Merritte who died at the age of 6 from hydrocephalus.

In an equally famous experiment, under the supervision of Watson, Jones (1924) aimed to remove the fears of a young child called Little Peter.

The Case of Little Peter (1924)

An orphan, Peter was 2 years and 10 months old when Jones and Watson began to study him. He was afraid of a white rat, and this fear extended to a rabbit, a fur coat, a feather, cotton wool, etc., but not to wooden blocks and similar toys. A rabbit was placed in a wire cage in the room where Little Peter ate lunch. Each day, the rabbit in the cage was brought a little nearer to Peter who eventually ate his lunch whilst nursing the rabbit on his lap.

Although it was never clear how Peter acquired his phobia, this experiment provided the first evidence that fears could be treated using a process of *systematic desensitization* (see below). This approach is popularly used by psychiatrists and psychologists in the treatment of phobias.

Definition

Systematic desensitization works on the principle that fear triggered, for example, upon seeing a spider, can be reversed or unlearned. The person is first taught relaxation exercises, and then shown a picture of their feared object (such as a spider). Over a period of time, they are introduced to a real spider. It is believed that relaxation will cancel out fear.

Based on the success of his experiments, Watson famously declared:

> Give me a dozen healthy infants, well-formed, and my own specified world to bring them up in and I'll guarantee to take any one at random and train him to become any type of specialist I might select – doctor, lawyer, artist, merchant-chief and, yes, even beggar-man and thief, regardless of his talents, penchants, tendencies, abilities, vocations and the race of his ancestors. (1928, p. 82)

Exercise

How might a child's early years experiences shape their behaviour?

Drawing on your experience, can you think of a child who displayed challenging behaviour when they first arrived at your setting? Did the child's behaviour change over time or was it resistant to change? Does Watson's theory account for continually challenging and resistant behaviour?

Undoubtedly, classical conditioning theory does explain some aspects of learning. You may have noticed the similarities between Watson's theory and Locke's seventeenth century philosophy of learning. Locke described the child's mind at birth as a blank slate (*tabula rasa*). Locke and Watson appear to share the notion that the child's outcome – whether they become a beggar or a king – is totally determined by life experience. In essence, both view the learner as a passive rather than an active participant in the learning process. Watson's theory was a major influence in education. Throughout the 1940s, 1950s and into the 1960s, teachers were more concerned with right answers than with children's understanding. Many adults will remember being taught their times tables by rote and the alphabet as a string. Without understanding, a person taught by rote will have to recite the full table until they get to the desired answer.

LEARNING THROUGH TRIAL AND ERROR

Edward Thorndike (1874–1949)

An American psychologist, Thorndike was born on 31 August 1874 and was one of the first pioneers of active learning, a theory that proposes that children should be encouraged to learn by themselves rather rely on teachers for instruction. Unlike the other theorists discussed in this chapter, Thorndike was a teacher educator not a scientist. He believed that trial and error learning constitutes the most basic form of learning. According to the Law of Effect, connections between actions and outcomes are strengthened in the presence of a reward. Thorndike famously identified the Halo effect (1920). According to this theory, an attractive child will be viewed as more intelligent, pleasant and kind than a less attractive child.

Although he accepted the principles of classical conditioning, Thorndike (1898) believed that the majority of learning was acquired through trial and error. He believed that when the outcome is positive connection (habit) is formed and the behaviour respected. Thorndike devised a puzzle box experiment to test the laws of learning. He placed a hungry cat in a box in clear view of a fish.

The cat's task was to escape from the box and get the fish. Each time the cat escaped, it was returned to the box. At first, trial and error secured the cat's release. Over time, the escapes became faster as the cat made a connection between its paw movements and the door lever. Thorndike termed the process which started with random acts and then became quite deliberate the *Law of Effect*. He believed that acts which produce negative consequences weaken and disappear, whereas acts which produce pleasurable outcomes are strengthened and maintained. Trial and error undoubtedly explains an aspect of learned behaviour – consider the following examples:

Jay (aged 3 years and 9 months) wants the sweets her mummy keeps in the sweetie cupboard beyond her reach. Jay stretches as high as possible but can't reach the cupboard. She tries to climb onto the work top but doesn't quite make it. Finally, she drags over a chair. She climbs on the chair then onto the worktop. Finally, by stretching, she reaches the cupboard but because the door opens out, she topples as she almost achieves her goal. Jay has shown insightful goal-directed behaviour. To get to the sweets, she tried a number of strategies but the negative consequence of falling and hurting herself make it unlikely that she will attempt this again – at least not in the near future.

Kyle (aged 4 years and 5 months) wants to take the fairground ride through the Haunted House. His daddy reminds him that the last time they went Kyle became very scared and was sick. Kyle insists that he was little the last time and now he is a big boy and won't be scared. At the end of the ride, Kyle is screaming and crying about seeing the ghosts. Later, he tells his mummy that the ride was good and he wants to go on it again.

Given the complexity and perverseness of human nature, the notion that behaviour producing negative consequences always weakens and disappears may be simplistic. Moreover, if all inappropriate behaviour could be reversed, then there would be no further need for behavioural units in schools, young offender centres or prisons. Similar to Pavlov and Watson, Thorndike was more concerned with explaining the laws of learning than in understanding how thinking, motivation and intentions affect behaviour.

BEHAVIOUR HAS CONSEQUENCES

B.F. Skinner (1904–1990)

An American psychologist, Skinner was born on 20 March 1904 in Pennsylvania. Married with two daughters, Skinner's research was heavily influenced by the work of Thorndike. He disagreed with the tenets of classical conditioning which portrayed the learner as a passive recipient of knowledge. He agreed with Thorndike's theory that individuals are not passive but active learners whose behaviour is shaped and maintained by rewards or punishments (consequences). His techniques continue to inform child behaviour programmes (such as star charts) and interventions for children with autism, elective mutism and problem behaviour.

Although he did not reject the work of Pavlov and Watson, Skinner believed that learning was not the passive process described in classical conditioning but an active process. In contrast to classical conditioning, in operant conditioning it is the learner not the object or trigger that produces changes in behaviour.

Definition

Operant conditioning (also referred to as instrumental conditioning) learning occurs when behaviour is either rewarded or punished. Through operant conditioning, an association is made between a behaviour and its consequences.

Consider Cody, a 3-year-old boy, who wants a biscuit. Rather than passively wait until it is provided, Cody starts by asking his mum, and when that fails he cries and stamps his foot. When that fails, he drags a chair over to the worktop, climbs up, opens the biscuit barrel and gets his reward.

Skinner concurred with Thorndike's belief that pleasant responses can strengthen a behavioural response and unpleasant responses can weaken and diminish behaviour. Skinner described the learning process as follows. Firstly, positive reinforcement

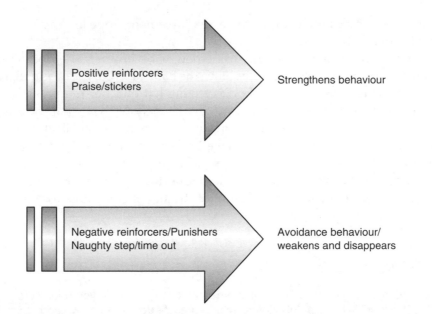

Figure 3.2   Positive and negative reinforcers

(such as praise, smiles, pats on the back, stars, etc.) strengthens behaviour. Secondly, negative reinforcers or punishers (such as the naughty step and time out) can discourage certain behaviours (see Figure 3.2).

Another important aspect of Skinner's work concerned the frequency of reinforcement. For example, if a child is praised every time they say thank you, the praise soon loses value. Rarely praised and the child may feel undervalued and stop saying thank you. In both cases, the behaviour weakens over time and disappears. Findings from his experiments with animals led Skinner to identify four reinforcement schedules. Illustrated in Table 3.1 below, using please as an example, it can be seen that once behaviour is established, rewards given on an intermittent/variable schedule have the greatest effect. Whilst continuous reinforcement might be useful at the start

Table 3.1   Reinforcement schedules and likely outcomes

Reinforcement	Pattern of praise	Likelihood of repetition
1 Continuous	Praise given at each utterance	Low/moderate
2 Fixed ratio	Praise fixed e.g. 4th/6th time	Low/moderate
3 Fixed interval	Praise given if please is said within a fixed time period e.g. 10 mins	Low/moderate
4 Intermittent/ Variable	Praise follows no set pattern e.g. 3rd/8th/11th	Moderate/high

of the process, intermittent or variable reinforcement appears to have a longer-lasting affect on behaviour.

Lori (aged 3 years and 2 months) has a new baby brother. She doesn't like him very much and would prefer a puppy. Since the baby arrived, Lori has had a number of temper tantrums. Worried that Lori is feeling left out, her mum asks if she will help bath the baby. Lori appears pleased and happily fetches a nappy, towel, baby bag and brush. Her mum repeatedly says what a good girl she is and because she has been such a good help offers to make Lori's favourite tea. The same activity is repeated every day until the fourth day when Lori lies down on the floor and screams that she doesn't want to be a helper. Continuous praise has lost its meaning and her mum will have to think of another strategy if she wants to improve Lori's behaviour.

Exercise

If Lori's mum asked you for advice, what practical strategies would you suggest to improve Lori's behaviour? What type of reinforcement schedule do you think would help to shape and maintain Lori's behaviour?

In the 1950s, Skinner took his research a step further by applying the principles of operant conditioning to computer assisted learning (CAL). Using a simple teaching package, he rewarded right answers with, for example, a star or 'well done' on screen, whilst a wrong answer received a 'try again'. Although CAL failed to gather support in the 1950s, by the 1990s the principles of operant conditioning were informing a number of therapeutic approaches used with, amongst others, disaffected children – children for whom school holds no point (Davies, 2008) – and children with autism (Silver and Oakes, 2001).

Popular approaches include the token economy and Applied Behavioural Analysis (ABA). Many schools employ an inducement scheme in the form of tokens to reward school attendance, good time keeping, neatness and good work. Pupils can exchange the tokens for prizes such as cinema tickets. As the pupil's behaviour improves, rewards are slowly replaced by verbal praise and eventually good grades. The token economy was devised by Ayllon and Azrin (1968) who used tokens to reinforce appropriate behaviour in 84 long-stay patients in a psychiatric hospital. Tokens were exchanged for meals, passes to leave the hospital or to buy better accommodation. To ensure the patients were clear about the expectations of staff, an explanation was given to patients who failed to win a token – for example, 'you don't earn your appearance token today … your hair is all tangled' (Gross, 1996, p. 832). Despite the success of the programme, there has been little increase in the use of the token economy in psychiatric hospitals.

Similarly, ABA, developed by Lovaas in 1987, aims to systematically reinforce appropriate forms of behaviour in children with autism. The programme involves teaching linguistic, cognitive, social and self-help skills across all settings and breaking down these skills into small tasks which are taught in a highly structured and hierarchical manner. There is a focus on rewarding, or reinforcing, desired behaviours and ignoring, re-directing or otherwise discouraging inappropriate behaviours. Lovaas recommended introducing a child with autism to an ABA programme before they reached 5 years of age. In addition, he devised a modified version of ABA in the form of play therapy for children aged 3 years and under. According to Keenan, Kerr and Dillenburger (2000), ABA has proven particularly affective in the treatment of young children with autism and has served to reduce stereotypical and disruptive behaviours before they become established.

Exercise

Identify the positive reinforcers used in your setting to shape and maintain appropriate behaviour. What negative reinforcers are used in your setting to stop inappropriate behaviour? What reinforcement schedules are favoured in the setting?

Advertising campaigns also exploit the concept of associated learning. For example, in television advertisements, chocolate is rarely featured without an attractive young woman shown eating it in a relaxed pose. Repeated exposure leads the audience to develop an association between the brand product and relaxation. This association can *generalize* to the extent that all forms of chocolate become associated with relaxation. Other marketing campaigns target different associations. For example, in advertisements for products such as toothpaste, the central character is frequently seen in a white laboratory coat. This suggests to the audience that this product has the support of experts in the field. Lifestyles are created with beautiful characters portrayed and it seems highly likely from the advertisement that if you use a certain brand of tinned corn that your children will wolf it down so that they will grow up to become big and strong.

Exercise

Identify the similarities and differences between classical and operant conditioning. Identify examples of both learning theories. Which, if either, best explains learning?

 ## Summary

This chapter has sought to familiarize students with two key learning theories termed classical and operant conditioning. Pavlov's discovery that dogs associate laboratory assistants with food causing them to drool provided the first systematic testable evidence about how learning is acquired. Watson applied Pavlov's principles of classical conditioning to humans and found it was possible to create or remove fears and phobias. The principles of systematic desensitization continue to be widely used. Whereas Pavlov and Watson viewed the learner as a passive recipient of information, Skinner believed that learning is an active process. In operant conditioning behaviour is believed to be shaped and maintained by its consequences. Similar to Thorndike, Skinner believed that negative rewards weaken negative behaviour and positive rewards strengthen positive behaviour. The principles of operant conditioning are practised on an almost daily basis in classrooms throughout the developed world. Star charts are frequently used to encourage good behaviour, whereas time out, withdrawal from an interesting activity and the naughty corner is used to discourage naughty or inappropriate behaviour. These principles have also been applied in work with children with autism and elective mutism. On the one hand, proponents of behaviourism would point out that, for more than 50 years, behaviourism had a major influence on the content and delivery of education in the western world. It also provided a platform for other theorists to develop their own theory of learning. Critics, on the other hand, would note how behaviourists failed to consider the complexity of human thought, motivation, intention or the social context on learning. For example, the perversity of human behaviour – taking a roller coaster ride when it makes you sick – can not be explained by behaviourism. The impact that covert processes such as thinking, intentions, motivation and understanding exert on learning are explored in the following chapters.

Table 3.2   Classical and operant conditioning: similarities and differences

Similarities	Differences
Both believe that learning is based on associations. This is often termed stimulus–response.	In classical conditioning, the learner is perceived as passive in the learning process.
Both explain aspects of learning.	In operant conditioning, learning is based on an association between behaviour and its consequences. A child will work hard for a reward and try to avoid punishments.
Both employ experimental, laboratory-based methods.	
Neither theory considers the role of creative or insightful problem solving in learning.	In classical conditioning, the learner is passive. Learning happens to rather than with the learner.
Neither considers the impact intentions, beliefs or experiences have on learning.	In operant conditioning, the learner is thought to be an active participant in the learning process. The learning is voluntary (if the task is too difficult, the child will stop even when a reward is offered).

Table 3.3   Behaviourism time lines and biographies

Ivan Pavlov
1849–1936
Classical Conditioning

A Russian physiologist, Pavlov was born on 14 September 1849 in the village of Ryazan.

His work on dog salivation led him to develop a theory of conditioned reflexes. Pavlov's theory, termed classical conditioning, has had a major influence on the field of psychology.

John B. Watson
1878–1958
Classical Conditioning

An American psychologist, Watson was born on 9 January 1878 in North Carolina. Inspired by the work of Pavlov, Watson applied the principles of classical conditioning to children. He founded a new school of thinking, 'behaviourism', in 1913.

Edward Thorndike
1874–1949
Law of Effect

An American psychologist, Thorndike was born on 31 August 1874. Thorndike was one of the first pioneers of active learning. He believed that trial and error learning constitutes the most basic form of learning.

B.F. Skinner
1904–1990
Operant Conditioning

An American psychologist, Skinner was born on 20 March 1904 in Pennsylvania. Skinner was influenced by the work of Thorndike. He agreed that individuals are not passive but active learners whose behaviour is shaped and maintained by rewards or punishments (consequences).

RECOMMENDED READING

Gross, R.D. (2010). *Psychology*: *The Science of Mind and Behaviour*, 6th edn. London: Hodder Education.

In its sixth reprint, this is a core text which offers students a thorough introduction to classical and operant conditioning. Primarily written for psychology students, the language is straightforward and examples are provided to ensure understanding.

REFERENCES

Ayllon, T. & Azrin, N.H. (1968). Reinforcer sampling: a technique for increasing the behaviour of mental patients. *Journal of Applied Behavioural Analysis. Spring, 1, 1,* 3–20.

Beck, H.P., Levinson, S. & Irons, G. (2009). Finding Little Albert: a journey to John B. Watson's infant laboratory. *American Psychologist, 64, 7,* 605–14.

Davies, M. (2008). Disaffected school children would be better off at work. *The Independent,* 13 November.

Gross, R.D. (1996). *Psychology*: *The Science of Mind and Behaviour*, 3rd edn. London: Hodder Arnold, H & S. Hooks.

Jones, M.C. (1924). A laboratory study of fear: the case of Peter. *Pedagogical Seminary, 31,* 308–15.

Keenan, M., Kerr, K.J. & Dillenburger, K. (2000). The way ahead. In M. Keenan, K.J. Kerr & K. Dillenburger (eds) *Parent's Education as Autism Therapists: Applied Behaviour Analysis in Context*. London: Jessica Kingsley.

Silver, M. & Oakes, P. (2001). Evaluation of a new computer intervention to teach people with autism or Asperger syndrome to recognize and predict emotions in others. *Autism, 5,* 299–316.

Thorndike, E.L. (1920). A constant error in psychological ratings. *Journal of Applied Psychology, 4,* 467–77.

Watson, J.B. (1928). *Psychological Care of Infant and Child*. New York: W.W. Norton Company, Inc.

4 PIAGET, LEARNING AND COGNITIVE CONSTRUCTIVISM

This chapter aims to:

- familiarize students with Piaget's theory of cognitive development
- illustrate this theory using practical examples
- highlight the strengths and weaknesses of Piaget's theory.

Jean Piaget (1896–1980)

Jean Piaget was a Swiss scientist, who was born in Neuchâtel (Switzerland) on 9 August 1896. A precocious and brilliant child, he wrote his first paper at the age of 11 on an albino sparrow. He continued to write and study throughout his life time, producing more than a hundred papers and books. Having studied the natural sciences at university, in later life Piaget developed an interest in psychoanalysis and intelligence testing. His research in developmental psychology and genetic epistemology had one unique goal: to understand how knowledge grows. Piaget is best known for his research on children's cognitive development which drew heavily on his observational studies of his infant children. He is credited with providing the first evidence that children's thinking is qualitatively different from adults' thinking.

INTRODUCTION

For almost 50 years, behaviourism – the school of thought that embraces classical and operant conditioning theories – (discussed in Chapter 3) – remained a dominant force in education. Classroom teaching was based on rote and drill (rote and drill involves the repetition of times tables, spellings, etc.) in the belief that this would promote learning. Using these approaches, teachers could test children's memory for facts such as the letters of the alphabet, colours, spelling and multiplication tables. Critical of the behaviourist approach, Piaget argued it merely encouraged the repetition of 'meaningless strings' and 'circus tricks' but failed to promote under-standing (Piaget, 1952). He favoured discovery learning through practical activities. Consider Jack who at 3 years 2 months is learning his colours at nursery. Every day the teacher sets up a row of coloured blocks and has Jack repeat the colours with her before she asks him to point to the red or yellow block. Despite doing very well on this task, observations of Jack show he has not learned his colours. Playing with his friend Sam, Jack holds up a car and asks 'Is that the blue one or the green one?' His friend considers and then tells him 'It's blue. My daddy has a blue car so I know it's blue.' The teacher realizes that Jack has merely repeated the words without connect-ing the colours with their name. In the following weeks, Jack's teacher introduces a number of games and activities aimed at reinforcing children's knowledge of colour. She links stories with colour and introduces a colour table which changes each week. Within a short time, Jack is observed talking confidently about colours.

In 1953, Piaget published *The Construction of Reality in the Child*. In this book, Piaget described the child as a lone scientist who creates his or her own sense of the world. According to Piaget, knowledge is constructed by the knower based on mental activity. His theory termed constructivism (a theory of knowledge that argues that humans generate knowledge and meaning from an interaction between their experiences and their ideas) provided the first major challenge to behaviour-ism. The popularity of this theory grew from the fact that it offered one of the first theories about the emergence and development of children's thinking.

It is interesting to consider how a scientist with an interest in the natural world came to be known as 'the giant of the nursery' (Elkind, 1972). A promising student, Piaget found himself working for Theodore Simon, the co-author of one of the world's first intelligence tests. Working in Binet's laboratory on the standardization of test items, Piaget found the types of errors children made on test items more interesting than correct responses. He was convinced that the errors were age-related rather than random and believed they offered an insight into how chil-dren think and learn. This work led him to conclude that children's thinking is radically different from adult thinking and that younger children think differently from older children. These claims were considered revolutionary within their time. Many of Piaget's contemporaries refused to accept this notion and disputed claims that infants' thinking evolves and changes with age and experience. Ignoring the controversy, over a 50-year period Piaget continued to refine and develop his the-ory. In the course of his investigations, he drew on the work of James Mark Baldwin

(1861–1934), one of the first psychologists with an interest in the cognitive development of infants and children. The terms 'accommodation' and 'adaptation' which are frequently attributed to Piaget were originally coined by Baldwin.

Definitions

Accommodation: This involves changing or adapting an existing schema, concept or idea to embrace new knowledge. Piaget believed that children learn by adaptation, which includes assimilation and accommodation.

Assimilation: According to Piaget, 'assimilation is the integration of external elements into evolving or completed structures' (Piaget, 1970, p. 706). By this, he means that new information is added into existing schemas or categories. Assimilation is an active and selective process.

Scheme/schema: Piaget used the term scheme, most often referred to as a schema, to describe the basic unit of intelligent behaviour. It is an active process which sorts information into simple categories. Schemas are not fixed but evolve and develop with experience.

Equilibration: This involves the child finding balance between external (environmental) and internal thinking processes. Disequilibration is the result of a mismatch between the two.

Piaget eschewed the experimental laboratory methods favoured by the behaviourists. Instead, he observed the development of children (using his own three children as a starting point) in their natural environment and recorded the slightest change in their actions. He also listened carefully to the explanations children gave as they completed a series of tasks. Piaget believed that children's thinking begins before they have the language to express their thoughts. Early thinking is more primitive and underdeveloped than later thinking and takes the form of schemes which encapsulate a number of schemas. For example, a baby aged between 4 and 8 months may have a scheme for shaking which incorporates a rattle schema or a shaky toy schema. Sutherland (1992, p. 33) explains Piaget's theory using the following analogy: 'just as a child's body's growth determines what size and shape of clothes he needs, so a child's thinking determines the language he needs'. Language, in Piaget's view, is merely a tool used to develop and enhance thinking. He believed that early speech is an expression of the child's needs and desires and he termed it *autistic*. Autistic speech is replaced by egocentric speech. The latter verbalizes the child's actions and movements; for example, 'I am going to sit on the big chair with mummy'. As the child becomes more aware of social expectations, egocentric

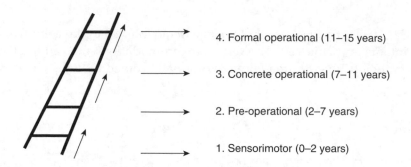

Figure 4.1 Piaget's stages of cognitive development

speech begins to fade and speech is internalized. Placing less importance on the development of speech than on cognitive development, Piaget interpreted this as evidence that the child was becoming less egocentric.

Two important trends underlie Piaget's theory of cognitive development. First, he believed that the child is powerfully and actively engaged in the learning process. Second, cognitive development follows a series of stages and substages. The stages and substages in Piaget's theory are invariant, meaning that each child must progress through each stage and substage in turn. They cannot skip a stage nor can they return to an earlier stage. If you imagine a child on the ladder above (see Figure 4.1), they start at the first rung and must move onto the next and the next until they have reached the top of the ladder. There is no stepping-off point and if you can picture a queue (knowledge and experience) building up behind the child then there is no going back. Another aspect of Piaget's theory which has been widely criticized concerns his claim that, irrespective of their culture or race, all children follow the same developmental pathway. The term universal is frequently used to sum this view.

THE SENSORIMOTOR STAGE (0–2 YEARS)

The first stage of cognitive growth is termed the sensorimotor stage. It derives its name from the early knowledge babies gain through their senses by sucking, shaking, grasping and observing. Piaget believed that newborns are incapable of thinking; instead they engage in reflexive activity. Most of these primitive reflexes are thought to be innate and include sucking and rooting reflexes. Using detailed observations of his own children, Piaget noted that, even in the first month of life, basic reflexes are modified by experience. For example, a young baby will continually turn its cheek until it locates the teat of a bottle. Within a few weeks, the baby's movements are less random and more deliberate, enabling it to locate the teat quickly. The sensorimotor stage is divided into six substages:

1 Reflexive (0–1 month)

   This is the most basic stage of development and is marked by simple reflexive activity such as grasping and sucking. Many of these reflexes are thought to be innate and essential to the baby's survival.

2 Primary circular (1–4 mths)

   Activities in this stage are centred on the baby's own body. They are called primary because they are the first motor habits to appear and circular because pleasurable activities tend to be repeated. This stage marks the emergence of relatively primitive schemas.

3 Secondary circular (4–8 mths)

   Activities in this phase are also repeated for pleasure. In contrast to the previous stage, the baby begins to notice interesting things happening in the environment. For example, having acciden-tally kicked the cot mobile, the baby watches it swing backwards and forwards. Although the baby may repeat this action several times, Piaget believed this was not intentional behaviour but discovered by chance.

4 Coordination of secondary schemes (8–12 mths)

   Intentional and planned behaviour begins to appear as the baby begins to manipulate the environ-ment. For example, the baby reaches for its bottle, puts it into its mouth and takes a drink. In linking these lifting and grasping movements, the baby begins to coordinate previously unrelated move-ments to achieve a goal. Object permanence begins to appear during this stage, meaning an infant understands that the toy hidden under the blanket has not disappeared but can be uncovered.

5 Tertiary circular (12–18 mths)

   Rather than repeat actions to create the same effect, infants begin to experiment to create their own effects. For example, having knocked over her baby cup, Nitta watches as the milk spills. Lifting the cup, she holds it upside down and then begins to shake it to make the milk pour out. This stage heralds the emergence of curiosity.

6 The beginning of representational thought (18–24 mths)

   This stage marks a significant shift in intellectual development. Problem solving begins to emerge through a combination of signs, symbols and mental imagery. Sitting in her car seat after a day at nursery, 2-year-old Lydia is observed opening and closing her fingers and moving them up and down as she mimes 'incy wincey spider' climbing up the spout.

The description of the sensorimotor stage provided by Piaget explains how, in two short years, an infant will progress from primitive reflexive movements such as grasping and sucking to become an experimental problem solver. The model fails, however, to explain the reason behind the transition from the sensorimotor to the pre-operational stage described below.

Exercise

Examine the six substages of the sensorimotor stage and consider why Piaget argued that each stage must be completed before an infant could progress to the next and that no stage could be missed.

Do you agree with this theory? Gather evidence to support your point of view.

THE PRE-OPERATIONAL STAGE (2–7 YEARS)

According to Piaget, an infant's thinking continues to develop throughout the pre-operational stage. As language develops, schemes become much more common. This stage of Piaget's theory has been criticized for focusing on the limitations of a young child's thinking rather than on their progress (Meadows, 1993). The pre-operational stage has two substages: the preconceptual phase (2–4 years) and the intuitive stage (4–7 years).

The preconceptual phase (2–4 years)

During the preconceptual phase, toddlers increasingly engage in imaginative and symbolic play. Symbols can be images or words that stand for something else, as reported in Piaget's observation of his infant daughter Jacqueline at play:

> At 21 months Jacqueline saw a shell and said 'cup'. After saying this she picked it up and pretended to drink … The next day, seeing the same shell, she said 'glass', then cup then 'hat' and finally 'boat' in the water. Three days later she took an empty box and moved it to and fro saying 'motycar'. (Piaget, 1962, p.124)

Observations of toddlers show they can now engage in make-believe play and imitate behaviour during this phase. Clip-clopping in high heels, Piers pretends to be a mummy going to the shops, while Jenna pretends she is a doctor looking after a sick child. For Piaget, play, particularly imaginative play, is an essential aspect of cognitive development. Thinking during this stage is, however, limited by a number of factors including egocentrism, animism, rigidity of thought and transductive reasoning. Each is examined in turn below.

Figure 4.2   The three mountain scene

Egocentrism

This refers to the child's inability to understand the world from another's point of view. For example, during a game of hide and seek, Ben who is 2 years and 4 months old covers his eyes with his hands. When Ben can't see others, he believes he can't be seen. Piaget demonstrated this theory using the 'three mountain scene' experiment depicted in Figure 4. 2 above (Piaget and Inhelder, 1956).

In this experiment, a child is first shown a cardboard mountain scene from a number of angles. A doll is placed opposite the child who is then asked to describe what the doll can see. The child can select the doll's viewpoint from a set of pictures. Throughout these experiments, young children consistently selected the picture that reflected their own view of the mountain scene. Based on evidence from a range of similar experiments with young children, Piaget concluded that during the pre-operational stage the young child has no sense of empathy (the ability to understand and identify with the feelings, thinking and motives of another) for another's feelings or thoughts.

Exercise

Drawing on your placement experience, can you think of a time when you saw a child show empathetic behaviour towards another child or to an adult? How does this experience relate to Piaget's theory of egocentrism?

Animism

According to Piaget, egocentrism pervades all aspects of the young child's thinking and is responsible for animistic thinking which ascribes feelings to objects. For example, every night, Josh aged 2 years and 8 months lines up his cars. He touches each one in turn, saying 'night, night. Sleep tight'. He lines them up together so they won't be lonely in the night. Piaget's claim that the pre-operational child is egocentric has been more heavily criticized than his other claims. His greatest opponent was Vygotsky (1986), followed by Donaldson (1978) and others.

Hughes (1978) tested Piaget's theory using a cross-shaped screen with a toy policeman positioned to the right of the child. To the left, a doll was hidden from the policeman but visible to the child. After training, nearly all of the children aged between 3½ and 5 years of age could correctly say when the policeman could and could not see the doll. Contrary to Piaget's assertion, Hughes concluded that children of this age can take another's perspective.

Donaldson (1978) was particularly critical of the questions Piaget asked children. She argued that they were phrased in such a way that they would catch children out rather than help them. Support for this notion comes from a more recent study into animism which showed that children have no difficulty understanding the difference between living things and objects when the word 'alive' is replaced with less ambiguous terms such as 'breathing' (Leddon et al., 2008). Leddon et al. concluded that the word 'alive' was masking children's understanding of the very concept under investigation.

Rigidity of thought and transductive reasoning

During the pre-operational stage, thinking is further limited by rigidity of thought and transductional reasoning. Rigidity of thought is the child's inability to reverse sequences and their inability to adjust to changes in appearance. For example, Deven is playing in the water tray. He watches Anya pour water from the red beaker into the blue beaker and back into the red beaker. When their teacher asks them which beaker has more water, both point to the red one. Their conviction is based on the fact that the red beaker is taller than the blue one. Children in the pre-operational stage have difficulty adjusting to changes in appearance. Using evidence from an experiment with pre-school children, Schaffer (2004, p. 176) illustrates this point. Pre-school children were shown a dog and asked to identify the animal. They correctly said it was a dog. While the children watched, a cat mask was placed over the dog's face. Asked to name the animal, most said it was a cat. Interestingly, each time the mask was removed and replaced, the children shifted from cat to dog.

Transductive reasoning occurs when a toddler makes inferences about relationships where there are none. For example, Carey has a baby in her tummy. Her tummy is very big and fat. Therefore, Melvin has a baby in his tummy because he has a big fat tummy. Joe's ball is round and the sun is round so Joe concludes that the sun is a ball. Transductive thinking begins to disappear at around the age of 4 (Lefrancois, 1995) but thinking in the latter part of the pre-operational stage remains intuitive rather than logical. Intuitive thought is based on perceptual attributes such as size and shape.

The intuitive phase (4–7 years)

This substage is only a slight advancement on preconceptual thinking. Children are getting better at seeing the whole scene rather than focusing on aspects of the scene. Piaget termed this ability 'decentring'. However, the child's thinking is limited by their inability to transfer their attention from the whole to the part and then back to the whole. In the example below, Orla begins by centering her attention on the whole group – paper plates – before focusing on a subgroup – colour.

Example

Four-year-old Orla is organizing plates into sets according to colour. Asked what she is doing, she explains that she is sorting paper plates into a yellow pile and a blue pile. Asked if there are more blue plates than yellow ones, Orla correctly points out that there are more blue ones. Asked 'are there more blue plates or paper plates?' Orla replies 'blue ones'. Having centred her attention on sorting by colour, Orla finds it difficult to transfer her attention back to the whole group – paper plates.

Piaget also believed that pre-operational children's understanding of conservation tasks is limited by their inability to move their focus beyond visual cues such as size and shape. In the conservation tasks illustrated below, (see Figure 4. 3), a child is shown

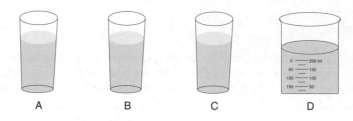

Figure 4.3   A water conservation task

two beakers of water and agrees that they contain the same amount of water. When one beaker of water is poured into a shorter but wider beaker, the pre-operational child argues that they are not the same and the taller beaker holds more water.

> **Definition**
>
> Conservation is the principle that quantities remain constant regardless of changes to their appearance.

Piaget believed that the ability to conserve marked the end of the pre-operational stage and the beginning of concrete operations. Children in the latter phase of the pre-operational stage ask endless questions and understand the difference between reality and fantasy. Critics argue that the end of Piaget's pre-operational stage is mainly defined by what children cannot do rather than by what they can do (Sutherland, 1992).

THE CONCRETE OPERATIONAL STAGE (7–11 YEARS)

The main difference between the pre-operational stage and the concrete operational stage is that children can now use logical rules to solve problems. According to Piaget, operational rules evolve gradually and sequentially as simple skills are consolidated, combined and reorganized into increasingly complex structures. Children are now able to reverse their thoughts when solving problems. This makes thinking more flexible and effective, though it is constrained by the child's need to have a concrete representation of mental thoughts. By way of example, Josh aged 7 is adding 6 + 9. First, he uses his fingers to count to 6 and then to add 9. He does this several times but keeps losing track of the numbers. Next, he uses a set of counters to help him and quickly works out that 6 + 9 = 15.

Seriation and transitivity are other hallmarks of the concrete operational stage. Seriation involves ordering objects or concepts according to a particular feature such as height, weight or speed. Closely related to seriation, transitivity is the ability to work out relationships such as: if Sean is younger than Jamie but older than Ashley, who is older than Ahmed, who is the oldest?

As previously mentioned, pre-operational children appear to have some difficulty in grasping the concept of conservation. While children are able to understand some forms of conservation, others prove more difficult. The water conservation task illustrated opposite involves the conservation of liquids and is understood by children of 6 and 7 years old. However, the conservation of weight is not seen until the age of 9, while the conservation of volume is not understood until the age of 11 (Piaget, 1969). Test your understanding of weight by considering the following: which is heavier – a ton of lead or a ton of feathers?

Understanding the conservation of volume involves recognizing that five ice cubes in a glass displace the same volume of water as one large ice cube of equal size and weight to the five. Acknowledging that some forms of conservation seem to be more easily understood than others, Piaget coined the term 'horizontal decalage' to explain developmental inconsistencies in children's learning.

Definition

Horizontal decalage: There are varying interpretations of the meaning of horizontal decalage; however, it can be understood as a term used to describe inconsistent performance on tasks involving similar mental operations. For example, a child might easily understand that there are 10 sweets in a line but not understand that there is the same number in a different configuration.

THE FORMAL OPERATIONAL STAGE (11–15 YEARS)

Having completed the first three stages, at approximately 11 years of age, a child progresses to the formal operational stage, which is the highest level of thinking. Piaget believed that the transition from the concrete to the formal operational stage takes place gradually over several years. Again, he failed to explain the reasons for this progression or why some children were more delayed or advanced than others.

This stage differs from the concrete operational stage in several ways. First, thinking is more flexible and there is less need for concrete props. Second, thinking

Figure 4.4   An illustration of horizontal decalage

is more symbolic. For example, in maths, understanding that a symbol can stand for a number becomes important in answering questions such as 'what is Y in the sum $3 \times X = Y$, if $X = 4$?' The answer is 12. Third, thinking is no longer constrained by personal experience or even reality. Children can begin to think about what they would like to do in the future. They can imagine what it would be like to have special powers or to live in a parallel universe. Fourth, thinking is logical and deductive. This enables the child to deduce what might happen if two elements are added together. For example, when direct heat is added to a magnesium strip, the magnesium burns and gives off a bright white light. A child will test theories in a more flexible and reflexive manner, noting the operations that do and do not work.

According to Sutherland (1992), Piaget failed to fully describe this last stage of development. Instead, it was left to neo-Piagetians (a group of researchers who sought to develop and refine Piaget's theory) such as Peel (1971) and Flavell (1963, 1977) to interpret his messages. Flavell, for example, described formal operations as a general orientation towards problem solving. Piaget never identified a stage past the formal operations, but several neo-Piagetians proffered a post-formal stage of operations to address some of the shortcomings of Piaget's theory (see Fischer, 1980). Perhaps due to the fact that a considerable number of adults never achieve the level of formal operational thinking described by Piaget, post-formal theories have failed to gain popularity. Given that the tasks used to measure formal operations focus on mathematics and science, critics point out that adults from societies which place less emphasis on these subjects will fail on tasks used to identify them as post-operational thinkers (Dasen and Heron, 1992). Similarly, adolescents taught in schools which focus on the arts or sports will do less well than budding scientists on these tasks. In later years, Piaget (1972) attributed these differences to the importance individuals placed on the tasks and argued that most people will solve at least one task. Nevertheless, Claxton (1998) remained highly critical of Piaget's emphasis on logical deductive thinking. He argued that this devalued other forms of thinking such as intuitive (an aspect of the pre-operational stage) and creative thinking.

SCHEMA FORMATION

Although there is some debate as to who first introduced the term schema, in his early work Piaget employed the word to describe 'general cognitive structures in children under the age of 5' (Athey, 1990/2003, p. 35). It was in his later work that Piaget drew a distinction between the terms schema and scheme. The former term he used to denote figurative thought and the latter operational thought. Figurative thought involves innate processes such as perception, memory and imagery. Piaget's concern was not however with these abilities but with their affect on problem solving and operational thinking (Chapman, 1999). He believed that schemas precede schemes and are the mental plans that inform action. Schemas are strongly visual. They help us to form impressions and identify inconsistencies in the environment. Look at the letters below; do you notice anything different in the example?

Although Piaget believed schemas are essential sources of information, they have the potential to bias our interpretation of facts and situations. Josh, for example, enjoys dressing up and likes the compliments he receives about his choice of dress. When he insists on wearing his sister's summer dress to nursery, he finds the reaction very different. Several of the boys laugh, point and call him

```
XXXXXXXXXXXXXXXXXXXXXXXXXXXXXXXXXXXXXXX
XXXXXXXXXXXXXXXXXXXXXXXXXXXXXXXXXXXXXXX
XXXXXXXXXXXXXXXXXXXXXXXXXXXXXXXXXXXXXXX
XXXXOXXXXXXXXXXXXXXXXXXXXXXXXXXXXXXXXXX
XXXXXXXXXXXXXXXXXXXXXXXXXXXXXXXXXXXXX
```

Figure 4.5   An illustration of schematic bias

a girl. The girls seem equally appalled that a boy is wearing a dress. Young children form a gender schema around the age of 18 months. At this age, they understand that they are a boy or girl and over the next year understand that their gender is fixed. Their gender schemas are primitive at this stage and hold stereotypical information about what it means to be a boy or girl, including appropriate clothing. Consequently, any breach of this code will be noted and cause a reaction.

For Piaget, schemas are concepts which evolve and develop through two complementary systems – accommodation and assimilation – using perception and memory to facilitate learning. Equilibration is achieved when internal and external events or information are in balance.

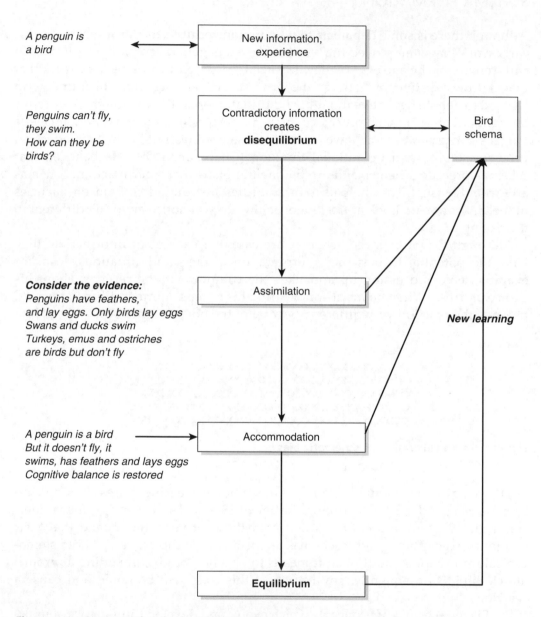

Figure 4.6   An example of schema formation

The example opposite (see Figure 4.6) draws on Lydia's (aged 4 years and 5 months) experience during a visit to the zoo. Watching the penguins, she described them as 'funny fish'. She was quite upset when told that penguins are birds. Pointing out that they don't fly but do swim, she concluded that penguins are fish. With help from her auntie, she searched the computer for evidence to support her notion that penguins are fish. Together, they discussed the fact that turkeys can't fly either and agreed that turkeys are birds, whereas swans and ducks swim and they are birds. A close-up picture of a penguin revealed its feathers and showed penguins sitting on nests to protect their eggs. The weight of evidence convinced Lydia, who achieved a stage of equilibration by assimilating and accommodating this new information into her bird schema.

Tracking and gazing are the first schemas to develop. At first, they are separate but become coordinated over time. Amir (aged 3 months) was observed on many occasions tracking the movements of the mobile hanging above his cot. Excited by the movement, he kicks out and accidentally touches the mobile making it swing backwards and forwards. This excites him more. Over time, Amir's movements become more purposeful and his kicking deliberate. His actions were initially informed by his tracking and gazing schemas.

Athey (1990/2003) identifies a number of schemas which denote specific behaviours. They include:

- dynamic vertical
- dynamic back and forth/side to side
- dynamic circular
- going over and under
- going round a boundary
- enveloping and containing space
- going through a boundary.

Many of these actions can be observed in children during the latter part of the sensorimotor stage or in the pre-operational stage. According to Hunt (1961), experience and an enriched environment are essential for the child to test and develop a repertoire of schemas.

Opportunities for the development of the dynamic vertical schema include activities involving height. Dylan (aged 1 year and 10 months) jumps off the bottom stair. He repeats this activity a number of times, shouting 'up, down'. Dylan is gaining a rudimentary understanding of height which will continue to develop.

The children in a playgroup session develop their understanding of tall and small when the staff draw around each child. They cut out each child's silhouette and then arrange them around the walls in order of height. Emma (aged 4 years and 3 months) is the tallest girl and Tanya (aged 3 years and 3 months) the smallest; George (aged 4 years and 8 months) is the tallest boy and Marc (aged 3 years) the smallest. Each child can compare their height with others in the class.

The dynamic back and forth/side to side can be seen in the play of Jack (aged 16 months). He toddles backwards and forwards between his play box and his nanny, each time bringing another wooden block. When nanny has all the blocks, Jack fetches stuffed toys. Although underdeveloped, these actions form the rudiments of a schema that will continue to develop over time.

Exercise

Using evidence from practise, identify examples of each of the following schemas: a dynamic circular; going over and under; and going round a boundary.

Given the opportunity, children will test out their ideas about space, capacity and volume, as illustrated in the examples below.

Example

Jenny (aged 3 years and 2 months) is playing with a toy bus. She fills the bus with toy people until there are no more seats left. She places the last two toy people beside the bus. Asked what she is doing, Jenny explains that the bus is full and there are no more seats so the people will have to wait for the next bus.

Kyle (aged 3 years and 8 months) is playing at the water tray. He fills the bucket with water and then pours it into a smaller bucket, watching as the water pours over the side. He repeats this action several times before filling the big bucket from the smaller bucket. He points to the bucket and tells his key worker 'there's still room. See the little bucket gets full but the big bucket it's got more room for water'. Kyle understands, though he doesn't have the vocabulary to explain, that the big bucket has greater capacity and holds a larger volume of water than the small bucket.

Highlighting the value of schema theory to early years practitioners, Nutbrown observes that:

What a schema is called is a way of labelling children's consistent patterns of action, and schemas are useful as an observational tool. They provide another way of looking at children, by giving focus to observational details which might otherwise become a list of disconnected events without much indication of learning or possible action to follow. Identifying a child's activities in terms of different schemas is only the first part in the process; the next step is to use detailed observations of children to decide how best to extend their learning. (2006, p. 7)

CRITICISMS OF PIAGET'S THEORY

Before examining further criticism of Piaget's theory, it is useful to keep in mind his contribution to our understanding of the developing child. He was the first theorist to attempt to explain the internal process of thinking. He offered researchers a range of new tools to examine the pre-verbal child's development including observations, detailed note taking and child-centred experiments. He placed the child at the centre of his studies and, in order to gain insight into their thinking, listened carefully to the answers they gave. Piaget was interested in process and how a child arrived at their final answer. In offering a model of how children's thinking develops, he advanced the growth of a new area of study, namely 'child development'.

Nevertheless, a number of criticisms have been levelled at Piaget's theory, particularly his claim that cognitive development happens in discrete stages. This theory has been widely disputed. In later years, Piaget (1970) modified the step-wise approach originally proposed in favour of a 'spiral' process of change. Using this analogy, Piaget described the process of intellectual development as an upward, expanding spiral in which children constantly reconstruct previously learned ideas. Despite these revisions, Piaget failed to explain why a child is driven to progress from one cognitive stage to another. Similarly, opponents argue that his theory of equilibration lacks clarity and is impossible to either prove or disprove (Sutherland, 1992).

The methods used by Piaget to investigate children's thinking have been the subject of considerable criticism. Meadows (1993), for example, argued that the language used in Piaget's experiments was too complicated for young children. She claimed that the wording was deliberate and chosen to 'catch children out' rather than to help them find the correct answer. Consequently, Piaget may have underestimated the child's ability to complete the task. Susan Isaacs was an early critic of Piaget's ideas, arguing that he tended to portray children in a negative light, emphasizing what they cannot do rather than what they can do (Isaacs, 1930). Another area of criticism concerns the small sample size employed in Piaget's research studies. The sample for Piaget's infancy research comprised his own three children. Although later childhood samples were larger, Piaget failed to record the exact numbers involved in his observations and tasks. Without a descriptive account of the children involved in his studies, Piaget has been accused of generalizing the results he gathered from samples of white, middle-class children with university-educated parents to children from other cultures and classes (Calloway, 2001).

Piaget's assertion that learning can never be accelerated has also been refuted. Meadows (1993) found it was possible to teach pre-school children to perform concrete operational tasks successfully three to four years ahead of time. Cognitive acceleration programmes such as those described by Shayer and Adey (2002) offer further evidence that it is possible to develop children's thinking. They had 5 year-old children participate in an activity with a teacher who asked them to sort a collection of dinosaurs into a T Rex pile and a blue pile. Cognitive conflict arises when a child has to decide where to place the blue T Rex. Using similarly challenging tasks, Shayer and Adey found it was possible to develop the child's cognitive ability. In a more recent study, Huntsinger et al. (2011) found differences in the creativity and drawing ability of Chinese and American children. Whereas Chinese parents believe that the essentials of drawing should be taught, American mothers believe it is an innate quality which will emerge naturally. Huntsinger et al. took samples of the children's drawing at 5, 7 and 9 years of age and found that at each age the Chinese children were more skilled at drawing and more creative than their American counterparts. Given the evidence base, it is unsurprising to note that countries in the developed world continue to fund early intervention programmes aimed at raising the educational standards of children, particularly these from disadvantaged areas.

Other than providing the child with a stimulating learning environment, Piaget's theory places little emphasis on the role of the teacher. By contrast, theorists such as Vygotsky (1978) and Bruner (1986) believe that teachers play a pivotal role in the development of the child's thinking and learning. Similarly, Vygotsky and Bruner take issue with Piaget's failure to consider the effect of culture and environment on the child's cognitive development. Consider, for example, an experiment conducted in a Mexican village where the native children made pottery to earn a living. When these children were tested using clay for conservation of mass, their answers were found to be significantly more advanced than those of their western counterparts (Price-Williams et al., 1969).

A final criticism concerns his proposition that learning involves schemas. Since this notion is purely hypothetical, it cannot be tested so is beyond refutation or verification. Similarly, the claims that information is assimilated and accommodated into existing schemas is argued to be vague and under-developed (Sutherland, 1992).

Exercise

Can you give an example of a young child who appears highly motivated to learn, a child who shows some motivation to learn and a child who appears to lack any motivation to learn? What might Piaget suggest can increase each child's motivation?

PIAGET IN THE EARLY YEARS SETTING

By the 1960s, enthusiasm for the chalk and talk approach favoured by behaviourists was fading fast as Piaget's theory of discovery learning gathered momentum. Children were no longer taught by rote and drill but allowed to discover facts for themselves with the help of a teacher who facilitated their learning. The physical environment changed as desks were organized into small groups rather than in rows facing the front of the classroom and children sat at child-sized furniture rather than at adult-sized desks. Whilst Piaget believed that teaching must be age-appropriate, in later years he accepted that some children progress at different developmental rates. Rather than focus on accelerating the child's learning, he encouraged teachers to examine the processes children use to arrive at their answers. By using this approach, a teacher could identify the child's stage of 'readiness' to learn. The concept of 'readiness' has generated a considerable amount of discussion in educational circles (Smidt, 2009). Given the notion that learning should be child-centred and tailored to meet the child's stage of readiness to learn, it is unsurprising to note that nursery teachers are the best customers of Piagetian messages (Sutherland, 1992). The similarities between Piaget's theory and the messages of Montessori (1949/1972), Froebel (1782–1852) and Dewey (1959) proved particularly popular with early years professionals. This was particularly true of their shared view that children learn best through practical activities, and that the role of the adult is to foster the child's inner drive, not impair it by imposing too many restrictions and obstacles in the child's environment. Both Dewey and Piaget believed that a child-centred teacher is a guide and an arranger of the environment, rather than an instructor. All of these theorists believed that teachers should provide the materials and activities that enable the young child to progress from discovery to discovery.

Another feature of Piaget's theory that proved popular with teachers was his emphasis on the role of peer interaction in the child's cognitive development. Corsaro (1992) defined the term 'peers' as a group of children who spend time together on a daily basis. Collaborative working on tasks which generate controversy, Piaget believed, enriches the child's communication skills and fosters intellectual development. His thoughts on the value of peer interaction are summed up in the following five points. First, children value the activities preferred by their peers. Second, peers can role model new concepts and skills. Third, a more able peer can explain an activity in simple terms to a learner. Fourth, the more able peer learns from verbalizing the problem. Fifth, both the learner and peer gain a greater insight into the problem through their shared learning experience. In the mid-1970s, a group of researchers explored the benefits of cooperative learning using a variety of concrete tasks which bore some similarity to Piaget's three mountain task. The children, aged between 5 and 7 years, first completed a task alone. One week later, half of the group again completed the task alone, while the other half completed it with peer. Doise et al. (1975) found that children who worked alone operated within the pre-operational stage, whereas those engaged in a shared learning experience tended to perform at the higher concrete operational stage. However, Piaget believed that a child's learning should not be accelerated. Instead, he advised teachers to engage children in stimulating tasks appropriate to their stage of development.

Although the popularity of Piaget's theory waned in the late 1970s, he retains a strong presence in the early years setting. For example, practitioners continue to ask open-ended questions that foster and develop the child's thinking. They observe children and focus on the process rather than on the output of learning. Rather than lead the child, practitioners continue to support and facilitate the child's learning. The introduction of the Foundation Stage curriculum in England and Wales in 2007 and in Northern Ireland in 2009 may be considered a late but welcome endorsement of the critical role of play in the child's social, emotional, physical and cognitive development, as previously proposed by Piaget.

Piaget's theory in action

Noting that it is snowing outside, a Year 1 teacher encourages the children to put on their outdoor clothes and together they go out into the snow. One group of children can be seen lifting the snow and throwing it, then squeezing it through their fingers before working it into snowballs to throw. Another group build a snowman, adding a nose, mouth, eyes, hat and scarf. The cold drives the children inside where they continue to talk about the snow and to draw pictures of snowflakes. The following day, some of the children are distressed to see that the snowman has begun to melt. The teacher takes them outside to gather snow in jars. Some children place their jars on their desks where they can watch it. Others place it on the heaters and a few place their jars in the freezer. Later, the children are fascinated to see that the snow in the jars on the heater and on their desks has melted into water but the snow in the freezer still looks like snow. Kelly asks the teacher if she can make the melted water into snow again: rather than answer, the teacher encourages Kelly to place her jar in the freezer. At the end of the day, they check the jar and Kelly and her friends see that the water has frozen and is now ice. The teacher asks Kelly what has happened and Kelly explains that she had 'snow first, then water and now ice'. She thinks about it and then decides that she has had 'lots of things but it's all water'.

Summary

Piaget described the child as a lone scientist who learns through practical experience. He viewed learning as a journey of discovery and was more interested in the process than the outcome. He was one of the first researchers to base his research on detailed observations of children, to use a diary to note small changes in infant development and to use interviews with older children to determine what they were thinking. Using this evidence, he devised a theory that children's thinking follows a step-wise three-stage approach, which he argued was invariant and universal. Each of the three stages outlined by Piaget must be completed before the child can progress to the final stage of formal operations. For Piaget, schemas are concepts which evolve and develop through two complementary systems – accommodation and assimilation. Equilibration is achieved when internal and external events or information are in balance. As children attempt to reduce the mental conflict caused by tension between what they know (their internal mental state) and external information, they develop and enhance their thinking. His theory fuelled interest in child development and led others to develop alternative theories. The concepts of equilibration and egocentrism have been the subject of considerable criticism. Similarly, Piaget's theory failed to consider the influence that individual differences, culture, environment, gender or motivation exert on the child's cognitive development. Whereas Piaget had no access to Vygotsky's work, Vygotsky was deeply influenced by Piaget's theory and proposed a theory which took account of the child's environment and culture. Vygotsky's theory is discussed in detail in chapter 5.

Included below, Table 4.1 summarises the strengths and weaknesses of Piaget's theory.

Table 4.1   The strengths and weaknesses of Piaget's theory

Strengths	Weaknesses
Adopts a child-centred approach. Children are viewed as active and powerful participants in the learning process.	
Posits a theory of cognitive development.	The theory is argued to be inflexible, rigid and to underestimate young children's ability.
	The theory fails to acknowledge the importance of culture, the child's environment, race, gender and motivation in the child's ability to learn.
	Terms such as equilibration lack clarity and are impossible to either prove or disprove.
Employs qualitative approaches including observations, listening to children as they complete tasks and interviewing children.	Lacks detail. Information concerning the participant groups is missing.
	The sample employed in observations was too small for the generalizations made by Piaget.
	Opponents claim that the questions posed in tasks are designed to catch 'children out'.
Is devised around a range of experimental tasks.	The tasks are argued to be complex and unfamiliar to the children.
	Wood (1998) pointed out that the vocabulary used in the tasks was too advanced for young children and caused them to fail.
	Egocentrism: research suggests that children are considerably less egocentric than Piaget believed (Donaldson, 1978).
Focuses on process rather than product.	
Recognizes the central importance of play.	
Highlights the importance of the child's 'readiness' to learn.	This suggests there is little an adult can do to enhance children's thinking.
	It assumes that readiness can be identified.
	As Duckworth (1987, p. 31) notes, in waiting for readiness a teacher is 'either too early and they [children] can't learn it, or too late and they already know it'.
	The concept of readiness ignores culture, race, gender and social and emotional differences.
Identifies the importance of peer interaction and collaborative learning.	
Affords the teacher a minimal role.	It gives the teacher a secondary role.
	It assumes that all children are capable of discovery learning without assistance or direction.
	Piaget tended to portray children in a negative light, focusing on what they couldn't do rather than on what they could do.

Table 4.2 below highlights the similarities and differences between Piaget's theory and behaviourism.

Table 4.2   Piaget and behaviourism: similarities and differences

Similarities	Differences
Theory: Pavlov, Watson, Skinner and Piaget posited ground-breaking theories of learning.	**Theory**: Piaget offered the first detailed explanation of the processes involved in detailed explanation about children's acquisition of learning.
Evidence base: They provided empirical evidence to support their learning theory.	**Education**: Piaget described children as lone scientists who are actively involved in their own learning. He viewed teachers as facilitators rather than instructors of learning. In contrast, behaviourists promoted a didactic chalk and talk approach to learning.
Child participants: Watson, Skinner and Piaget studied children's learning.	
Active participants: Skinner and Piaget believed that children were active participants in the learning process.	
Research: The theories posited by Pavlov, Watson, Skinner and Piaget fuelled interest in the development of learning. Research continues to examine the processes involved in the transmission and acquisition of learning.	**Process vs product**: Piaget was more interested in process than product.
Unpopularity: The behavourist theory, like Piaget, lost favour, though it remains an influential theory.	
Qualitative methods: Whereas behaviourists favour quantitative experimental methods, Piaget employed a qualitative approach to study child development. The methods included observations, interviews and listening to children as they completed tasks.	

RECOMMENDED READING

Athey, C. (1990/2003). *Extending Thought in Young Children: A Parent–Teacher Partnership*. London: Paul Chapman Publishing.

This useful text offers a very thorough discussion of schematic thinking. It includes a range of early years examples to ensure understanding and provides a detailed account of Piaget's contribution to current pedagogical thinking on schemas.

Nutbrown, C. (2006). *Threads of Thinking: Young Children Learning and the Role of Early Education*. London: Sage.

A favourite amongst early childhood students, Nutbrown offers further insight into schema formation. Material covered by Athey is reiterated in a different, and arguably, more accessible style with numerous early years examples included to illustrate theoretical points. The book continues by looking at the implications of a curriculum for thinking and the assessment of learning.

REFERENCES

Athey, C. (1990/2003). *Extending Thought in Young Children. A Parent–Teacher Partnership*. London: Paul Chapman Publishing.

Bruner, J.S. (1986). *Achial Minds, Possible Worlds*. Cambridge, MA: Harvard University Press.

Calloway, W.R. (2001). *Jean Piaget: A Most Outrageous Deception*. New York: NOVA.

Chapman, M. (1999). Constructivism and the problem of reality. *Journal of Applied Psychology, 20*, 31–43.

Claxton, G. (1998). *Hare Brain, Tortoise Mind: Why Intelligence Increases When You Think Less*. London: Fourth Estate.

Corsaro, W.A. (1992). Interpretative reproduction in children's peer cultures. *Social Psychology Quarterly, 55*, 160–177.

Dasen, P.R. & Heron, A. (1992) Cross-cultural tests of Piaget's Theory. In L. Smith (ed.) *Jean Piaget: Critical Assessments*. London and New York: Routledge.

Dewey, (1959). *School and Society*. Chicago, IL: University of Chicago Press.

Doise, W., Mugny, G. & Perret-Clermont, A.N. (1975). Social interaction and the development of cognitive operations. *European Journal of Social Psychology, 5, 3*, 367–83.

Donaldson, M. (1978). *Children's Minds*. Glasgow: Collins, Fontana.

Duckworth, E. (1987). *The Having of Wonderful Ideas and Other Essays on Teaching and Learning*. New York: Teachers College Press.

Elkind, D. (1972). Giant in the nursery – Jean Piaget. In R.F Biehler (ed.) *Psychology Applied to Teaching; Selected Readings*. Boston, MA: Houghton Miffin.

Fischer, K.W. (1980). A theory of cognitive development: the control and construction of hierarchical skills. *Psychological Review, 8, 2*, 477–531.

Flavell, J.H. (1963). *The Developmental Psychology of Jean Piaget*. New York: Van Nostrand.

Flavell, J.H. (1977). *Cognitive Development*. Englewood Cliffs, NJ: Prentice Hall.

Hughes, M. (1978). Selecting pictures of another person's view. *British Journal of Educational Psychology, 1*, 207–19.

Hunt, J.M. (1961). *Intelligence and Experience*. New York: Ronald Press.

Huntsinger, C., Jose, P.E., Kreig, D.B. & Luo, Z. (2011). Cultural differences in Chinese American and European American children's drawing skills over time. *Early Childhood Research Quarterly, 26, 1*, 134–45.

Isaacs, S. (1930). *Intellectual Growth in Young Children*. London: Routledge & Kegan Paul.

Leddon, E.M., Waxman, S.R. & Medin, D.L. (2008). Unmasking 'Alive': children's appreciation of a concept linking all living things. *Journal of Cognition and Development, 9, 14*, 461–73.

Lefrancois, G. (1995*). Theories of Human Learning*, 3rd edn. Pacific CA: Brooks/Cole.

Meadows, M. (1993). *The Young Child as Thinker: The Cognitive Development and Acquisition of Cognition in Childhood*. London: Routledge.

Montessori, M. (1949/1972). *Education and Peace*. Chicago, IL : Henry Regnery.

Nutbrown, C. (2006). *Threads of Thinking: Young Children Learning and the Role of Early Education*. London: Sage.

Peel, E.A. (1971). *The Nature of Adolescent Judgment*. London: Staples Press.

Piaget, J.P. (1952). *The Origins of Intelligence in Children*. New York: International Universities Press.

Piaget, J.P. (1953). *The Construction of Reality in the Child.* London: Routledge and Kegan Paul.

Piaget, J.P. (1962). *Play, Dreams and Imitation in Childhood.* Norton: New York.

Piaget, J.P. (1969). *Intellectual Operations and their Development.* New York: Basic Books.

Piaget, J.P (1970). *Science of Education and the Psychology of the Child.* New York: Orion.

Piaget, J.P. (1972). *To Understand is to Invert.* New York: The Viking Press, Inc.

Piaget, J.P. & Inhelder, B. (1956). *The Child's Conception of Space.* London: Routledge.

Price-Williams, D., Gordon, W. & Ramirez, M. (1969). Skill and conservation: a study of pottery-making children. *Developmental Psychology, 1,* 769.

Schaffer, H.R. (2004). *Introducing Child Psychology*. Oxford: Blackwell.

Shayer, M. & Adey, P. (eds) (2002). *Learning and Intelligence: Cognitive Acceleration Across the Curriculum from 5 to 15 Years.* Buckingham: Open University Press.

Smidt, S. (2009). *Introducing Vygotsky. A Guide for Practitioners and Students in Early Years Education.* Routledge: London.

Sutherland, P. (1992). *Cognitive Development Today: Piaget and his Critics.* London: Paul Chapman Publishing.

Wood, D. (1998). *How Children Think and Learn,* 2nd edn. Oxford: Blackwell.

Vygotsky, L.S. (1978). *Mind in Society: The Development of Higher Psychological Processes*. Cambridge, MA: Harvard University Press.

Vygotsky, L.S. (1986). *Thought and Language,* 2nd edn. Oxford: Blackwell.

5 VYGOTSKY: LEARNING IN A SOCIAL MATRIX

This chapter aims to:

- familiarize students with Vygotsky's theory of social constructivism
- illustrate this theory using practical examples
- highlight the strengths and weaknesses of Vygotsky's theory.

Lev Semyonovich Vygotsky (1896–1934)

Lev Vygotsky was born into a traditional Jewish family in Orsha (Belarus) in Russia on 17 November 1896, the same year as Piaget. He began his studies in medicine at Moscow University at a time when Jews suffered considerable discrimination. He transferred to Moscow's Law School before again changing course to study literature, art and philosophy at Shanavsky University in Moscow. After completing his dissertation on The Psychology of Art, he became a junior psychologist at the Psychological Institute of Moscow University. He later taught psychology at a local teacher training college where he formed a research 'troika' (threesome) group with Alexander Lauria and Alexie Leontiev. During his short lifetime, Vygotsky wrote more than 180 papers; some are only now being translated. Similar to Piaget, Vygotsky's focus was on child development. He is, however, credited with developing an approach that connects social and mental processes and describes cognitive development as an essentially social process. Vygotsky married and had two daughters. His daughter and granddaughter continue to develop his work.

INTRODUCTION

At its height in the late 1920s, Vygotsky's views about the mind were among the most influential in Russia. Such was the popularity of his work that it attracted the attention of the communist government who denounced it on the grounds that it was little more than bourgeois idealism which referenced the western theorists Freud and Piaget. Vygotsky's work was subsequently banned by Stalin and confined to a single central library in Moscow, accessible only by special permission from the secret police. There it remained undiscovered by western theorists until the 1960s. Vygotsky's popularity soared and waned again in the 1970s only to emerge as a tour de force in the mid-1980s. Indeed, such was his renewed popularity that Toulmin (1978) described Vygotsky as 'The Mozart of Psychology'. You will notice that, although long dead, references to Vygotsky's work are cited as 1962, 1978, 1983, 1987–1998. These books and papers are recent translations of Vygotsky's original papers. Both Meadows (1993) and Daniels (2005) note that many of these translations are peppered with inaccuracies and misinterpretations and truncated (abbreviated) to exclude all mention of Marxist philosophy. This is an important omission since it serves to contextualize and explain the influences that determined Vygotsky's views.

Mindful of these points, the information presented in this chapter is drawn from a large body of credible sources which seek to faithfully report Vygotsky's theory (including Daniels, 2005; Meadows, 1993; Schaffer, 2004; Smidt, 2009 and Sutherland, 1992).

VYGOTSKY AND SOCIAL CONSTRUCTIVISM

According to social constructivist theory, it is important to consider the quality and nature of the child's environment, their age, culture and life experiences before drawing any conclusions about their development.

> **Definition**
>
> **Constructivism:** An approach to teaching and learning based on the premise that cognition is the result of mental construction.

Vygotsky believed that all aspects of learning have a history based on real-life experiential learning, much of it learned before a child ever starts formal education. In keeping with his theoretical perspective, Vygotsky never proposed a theory of child development. Schaffer notes that:

> The only statement he made about age was to suggest that children up to 2 years are influenced primarily by biological forces and that the socio-cultural influences which form the focus of his writings do not come into play until after that age – an assertion clearly not supported by more recent work. (2004, p. 201)

Similarly, his interest was never in the child as an individual but, reflecting his Marxist ideology, in the child as a member of their cultural context. According to Vygotsky, development is not an individual process but the result of an aggregate of social relations embodied within the individual. In order to understand the path and nature of child development, Vygotsky believed it is essential to examine the social context in which children develop (Tudge, 1992). He pointed out that children do not develop in isolation but in a social matrix. This social matrix is formed by the interconnection of social relationships and interactions between themselves and other children (Corsaro, 1992). Through these relationships and interactions, children collaborate towards a shared goal. Vygotsky's theory on the process of child development is summed up in the following comment:

> In the process of development, children begin to use the same forms of behaviour in relation to themselves and others initially used in relation to them. Children master the social forms of behaviour and transfer these forms to themselves ... it is through others that we develop into ourselves and ... this is true not only with regard to the individual but with regard to the history of every function. (in translation, Wertsch, 1981, p.164)

Like Piaget, he believed that infants are born with the basic building blocks of cognition: these include visual recognition, memory, attention and speed of processing. This enables the child to develop higher order thinking skills such as problem solving, reasoning, planning and remembering (Rose et al., 2003). The child also has an innate ability to learn through instruction, a characteristic complemented by the adult's willingness to help and instruct. Thus, the cultural norms (accepted practices) of a society begin at the external level and, through experience and mediated learning, become internalized as thought.

> Every function in the child's cultural development appears twice: first, on the social level, and later on the individual level; first, between people (interpsychological), and then inside the child (intrapsychological). This applies equally to voluntary attention, to logical memory, and to the formation of concepts. All the higher functions originate as actual relations between human individuals. (Vygotsky, 1978, p. 57)

Exercise

Consider the above quote carefully. What does Vygotsky mean when he claims that learning involves two levels: a social and an individual level?

CULTURE AND SOCIETY

As previously suggested, Vygotsky's life and views were shaped by the social and political forces which revolutionized Russia. Vygotsky was particularly interested in supporting children with special educational needs and sought to explain the social and educational inequalities of the time. Similar to his contemporary Piaget, he believed that children are active constructors of their own knowledge and skills. In contrast to Piaget, however, he believed that child development is the result of interactions between the child and their social environment. Consider, for example, Julie (aged 3 years and 2 months) who is pretending to be a contestant on the X Factor TV talent show. She is frustrated because she cannot work the toy microphone. She shakes it and bangs it before throwing it down. Clare (a playgroup assistant) picks it up and asks 'has it got batteries?' Turning it over in her hands, she points out that 'it's not switched on'. Passing the microphone back to Julie, Clare shows her how to switch it on and then encourages Julie to have a go. Clare further extends Julie's play by inviting Matthew and Cody Lee who have been watching this exchange to be judges with her on the X Factor panel while Julie sings.

Both Piaget and Vygotsky would agree that the collaborative interaction taking place in this scenario is extending Julie's knowledge of how a microphone works. As a social interactionist, Vygotsky would also note the shared cultural experience which underpins this interaction. Here, no explanation of this popular talent show is required; everyone involved is familiar with the programme and understands the roles involved. Reflecting Vygotsky's belief that children are not solitary constructors of their knowledge but members of their prevailing culture, he observes how social interaction can involve parents, siblings, peers, teachers and significant objects such as books or favourite toys. Each, he argued, provides the cultural tools necessary to develop the child's thinking.

Definitions

Social constructivism: Social constructivism emphasizes the importance of culture and context in understanding what occurs in society and constructing knowledge based on this understanding (Pagram and McMahon, 1997).

> **Culture**: This is a complex concept. Put simply, it involves the socially transmitted behaviour patterns, arts and beliefs passed from one generation to another.
>
> **Cultural tools**: These are the products of human cultural and historical activity.

Whilst cultural tools such as nursery rhymes, fairy stories, music and art become so familiar as to be invisible, Vygotsky was keen to acknowledge their role in the development of thinking. His views on the importance of cultural tools are best summed up in the following quote from Pea who notes that:

> these tools literally carry intelligence in them, in that they represent some individual's or some community's decision that the means thus offered would be reified, made stable as quasi permanent, for the use of others. (1993, p.52)

Consider the following examples:

Examples

1 Dylan (aged 1 year and 10 months) is observed lifting his daddy's mobile phone and holding it to his ear, shouting 'hello, hello'. Later, he points the phone at the television; pressing several buttons as he tries to change channels.
2 Every morning, Anelisa (aged 3 years) and her sister Miriam (aged 5 years and 2 months) fetch drinking water from the stream (two miles away) using plastic containers left by relief workers. The containers are light, have handles and are easy for the girls to carry.
3 Saturday is library day and Lita (aged 5 years and 6 months) is excited. She is hoping to borrow the book recommended by her friend Raine, *The Princess Mouse: A Tale of Finland*. While Lita searches the shelves, her mummy watches from the coffee shop and chats to her friends. Lita can't read and doesn't start her formal education until she is 7 years old but she enjoys meeting friends at the library.

In brief, cultural tools influence our perception, understanding and experience of the world. For Vygotsky, lower order thinking involves unconscious biological functions such as memory, attention and intelligence. These processes are not value-free and are influenced by our feelings and emotions. Since lower order functions are linked by biological, social, affective and cultural factors, Vygotsky termed them *psychobiological functions*. In contrast, higher order functions involve conscious deliberate intentions and actions – for example, problem solving and logical reasoning. Mediated, social, collaborative activity can be thought of as the bridge which brings a child from lower order concrete thinking to higher order abstract thinking.

Lower order thinking   *Higher order thinking*

Thoughts   ⎫   Attention   Mediated social   Problem solving

Feelings   ⎬   Memory   collaborative activity   Logical reasoning

Values   ⎭   Intelligence   Abstract thinking

Figure 5.1   Bridging lower and higher order thinking

> **Exercise**
>
> Look at Figure 5.1 above. Consider how thoughts, feelings and values might affect a child's attention, memory and intelligence. Would these factors have any impact on a child's ability to problem solve, think logically, reason or think abstractly?

DEVELOPING LANGUAGE AND THOUGHT

Language is another cultural tool which Vygotsky believed mediates thinking and learning. He described it as 'a powerful and strong tool' in children's interactions. As children listen and respond to each other's ideas and contributions, they develop and enhance their own understanding (Tudge and Winterhoff, 1993). For Vygotsky, language plays a central role in the development of cognition:

> The structure of speech is not simply the mirror image of the structure of thought. It cannot, therefore, be placed on thought like clothes off a rack. Speech does not merely serve as the expression of developed thought. Thought is restructured as it is transformed into speech. It is not expressed but completed in the word. Therefore, precisely because of the contrasting directions of movements, the development of the internal and external aspects of speech forms a new unity. (Vygotsky, 1987; cited in Holzman, 2006, p. 115)

Although this aspect of his work was incomplete, Vygotsky attempted to chart the developmental course of language. He believed that language carries meaning and sense and must be interpreted by the child. Through these interpretations, the child contributes to society and society to the child. It is the interactive reciprocal nature of these relationships which underpins social constructivism. Vygotsky's theory comprises four stages, starting with the pre-verbal stage and progressing to the internalization of speech as thinking. It is important to remember that, unlike Piaget, Vygotsky was offering a general theory not advocating a fixed and universal staged approach.

1 **Primitive stage**: Children under 2 years of age use vocal activity as a means of emotional expression and for social engagement. Non-verbal gesturing is not unusual during this stage as behaviour becomes increasingly purposeful and goal-directed. At the primitive stage, thought and language are separate. Pointing and staring are not uncommon during this stage and are easily interpreted by a sensitive caretaker who uses language to reinforce non-linguistic communications. Bruner (1986) saw gesture and non-verbal cues as having an enormous impact on the later development of language.

   Josh (aged 18 months) wants his bottle. Babbling, he points to the bottle on the work top and stares at it until his mum notices, interprets and rewards his actions. Giving him the bottle, she confirms 'you want your bottle'.

2 **Practical intelligence**: During this stage, the child's language uses syntactic (rules of speech) and logical forms. These forms of speech are linked to the child's practical problem solving activities but are not linked in a systematic way (Meadows, 1993, p. 245).

   Maisie (aged 3 years and 2 months) has lost a piece of her jigsaw. She searches the table then under the table, then in her pockets. Kerry, her key worker, asks if she is looking for the piece sitting on top of the jigsaw. Maisie laughs and slots it into place. Maisie has some understanding of logical actions but at this stage her search tends to be unsystematic and a little haphazard.

3 **External symbolic stage**: Thinking aloud is common during this stage with language used to help with internal problem solving. The transition between external social speech and internal private speech is marked by egocentric speech – also termed thinking aloud. Thinking aloud enables the child to self-regulate and plan their activities. Although Vygotsky believed that social speech precedes egocentric speech, he agreed that speech does not always require an audience. For example, Katrina (aged 6 years and 4 months) is observed quietly counting on her fingers as she completes an exercise in class. She seeks the teacher's attention only to check her work.

4 **Internalization of symbolic tools**: Between 7 and 8 years of age, children internalize thinking and egocentric speech begins to disappear. Problem solving continues to be guided by speech but the voice is internal (thinking). This stage leads to greater cognitive independence, flexibility and freedom. Thought continues to be framed by internalized individual, cultural and societal norms.

Unlike Piaget, Vygotsky did not advocate a staged unidirectional approach to development. On the one hand, he believed that development is progressive and tends to follow an incremental pathway. On the other, he acknowledged that a child may move backwards or forwards between the stages outlined above as their thoughts mature. Problem novelty or difficulty can cause a child to regress to an earlier stage, whereas experience will progress development. It was the flexibility of his theoretical approach to how language development informs thinking that led Sutherland (1992) to conclude that Vygotsky's theory was decades ahead of its time.

PLAY, CREATIVITY AND THOUGHT

Vygotsky believed that imaginary play is a precursor to abstract thinking. Through play children exercise their understanding of objects, develop relationships, mimic adult behaviour and adopt fantasy roles. Vygotsky (1987–1998, p. 28) described play as 'self education'. Vygotsky's notion of the development of play parallels the work of Piaget. Both believed that infants as young as 12 months are capable of object substitution (using one object to substitute for another) but that it mainly occurs in the second year and, for Vygotsky, is initiated by adults. As with other social and cultural behaviours, play is mediated through the nursery rhymes, songs, stories and fables that denote the child's culture.

According to Vygotsky, children's play is not merely a process of repetition. While it begins in social interactions with adults, the child soon displays independent, pretend and creative play. During this latter phase, the child is beginning to develop autonomy and takes charge of their play experience. They become more confident and adventurous, and develop rules which they may share with their peers but which may exclude adults. Wood (2011), for example, observed children's play in a nursery playground over a period of time. Concerns had been raised regarding the children's failure to use the climbing equipment in the playground. In the course of her observations, Wood found that the children had invented their own game which excluded the Troggs (adults in the setting). The games had set rules with punishments included for violations. The children would sneak into the play house to hide from the Troggs but peep up every so often to see if they had been caught. If caught, the children imposed their own punishment which involved hopping through a set of tyres. The climbing frame was considered to be 'out of bounds' because it was visible to the adults in the setting.

Vygotsky would explain this behaviour as imaginative play predicated on a shared understanding of the rules. Vygotsky believed that imaginative play begins at the social level, then through the medium of language it becomes internalized as thought. By early adolescence, social and environmental props are no longer required to support fantasy and imaginative thought. Interestingly today, children and adults are less likely to abandon props and increasingly engage in fantasy play through the medium of computer games.

THE ZONE OF PROXIMAL DEVELOPMENT: WALKING A HEAD TALLER

The zone of proximal development (ZPD) is one of the most extensively referenced and least understood aspects of Vygotsky's work (Palinscar, 1998). Although it appears in only a few of the many thousands of pages Vygotsky wrote during his short lifetime, students tend to focus on this aspect of his work to the exclusion of others (Tudge, 1992). Murphy (2012) described the ZPD as a work in progress and notes that the term was initially used as an index for intellectual potential and later as an educational concept focusing on the conditions necessary to establish a ZPD. Vygotsky defined the ZPD as:

> those functions which have yet to mature but are in the process of maturing … 'buds' or 'flowers' of development rather than 'fruits' of development. The actual development level characterises the cognitive development retrospectively while the ZPD characterises it prospectively. (1978, p.86)

In order to provide tailored learning opportunities for children, Vygotsky believed it is necessary to establish two developmental levels (Meadows, 1993). The lower level provides a baseline measure of what a child can achieve independently on an ability test or task. The higher measure is the level the child can achieve with help and support. According to Vygotsky, the ZPD is:

> not a specific quality of the child, nor is it a specific quality of the educational setting or educators … it is … collaboratively produced in the interaction between the child and more knowledgeable others. The aim of this collaborative interaction is to lift the learner to become 'a head taller'. (Vygotsky, 1978, p. 102)

The child at the lower level of the ZPD is dependent on the teacher to guide and develop their learning. The adult is tasked with developing a self-regulated and increasingly competent learner. With this in mind, the adult's goal is to progressively reduce support as the child develops expertise. The child at the optimal level of the ZPD has achieved a degree of independence and ownership of their learning which renders further assistance unnecessary. At this point, new tasks and challenges can be identified to develop the child's learning further. Vygotsky believed that the ZPD offers a diagnostic tool to facilitate the development of a plan of learning to extend and support the learner. He acknowledged that individual children will require different levels of support and are capable of different levels of achievement. He asks the reader to imagine that:

> we have examined two children and we have determined that the mental age of both is seven years. This means that both children solve tasks accessible to seven-year-olds. However, when we attempt to push these children further in carrying out the tests, there turns out to be an essential difference between them. With the help of leading questions, examples and demonstrations one of them easily solves test items taken from two years above the child's level of development. The other solves problems that are only a half-year above his or her development. (Vygotsky, 1956 pp. 446–7)

Figure 5.2 illustrates the child's potential for improvement with support. The child's potential is determined by a knowledgeable adult such as a parent, early years professional or teacher who will strive to plan, monitor and develop the child's ability. Whilst it is important to help the child improve upon their current ability level, it is equally important that goals within the ZPD are achievable and realistic rather than unachievable and aspirational. Beyond the ZPD remain all the problems and tasks that the child has yet to encounter and which exceed the child's current ability level, even with support.

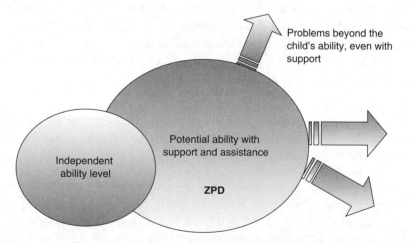

Problems beyond the child's ability, even with support

Potential ability with support and assistance

Independent ability level

ZPD

Figure 5.2   A schematic view of the zone of proximal development

Exercise

Consider the reasons why some problems or tasks may be beyond the child's current ability level, even with support?

Although he did not address the issue of individual differences in detail, Vygotsky clearly acknowledged that children are individuals with different levels of potential (see Figure 5.3 below). He pointed out that even when two children of the same age display a similar level of ability, their potential may be limited by personal or internal factors such as intelligence and motivation or by external social and environmental factors. In essence, Vygotsky believed that a knowledgeable adult will tailor a programme to suit the child rather than expect every child to rise to meet unrealistic goals. In the figure below, you will note that child A and child B both started with the same level of ability and with support both made improvements. Whereas child A went on to make significant gains, child B made modest progress. (see Figure 5.3 below).

In 1976, Wood, Bruner and Ross coined the term 'scaffolding' as a metaphor to explain the nature of the aid provided by an adult for a child who could not successfully complete a task alone. The concept arose from their observations of

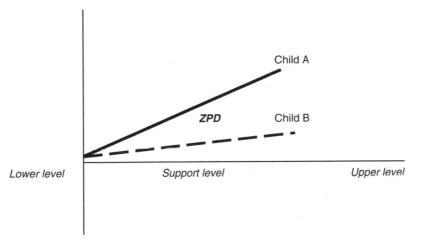

Figure 5.3   Individual levels of progress

the strategies mothers used to help their 3 to 4-year-old children complete a wooden block task. They noted that children were encouraged to complete as much of the task as possible alone before assistance was offered. Benson (1997) sums this view when he states that 'scaffolding is actually a bridge used to build upon what students already know to arrive at something they do not know; if scaffolding is properly administered, it will act as an enabler, not as a disabler' (p.126–7).

Consider the examples below.

Examples

Tia (aged 3 years and 6 months) enjoys jigsaws. She has a large collection of 10- and 15-piece jigsaws at home and is frustrated with the 'baby' 5- and 10-piece jigsaws available in nursery. To extend Tia's learning, her teacher sources a number of 20- and 25-piece jigsaws including Tia's favourites: Hello Kitty, Peppa Pig and the Disney princesses.

Alex (aged 4 years and 2 months) is making a spider for Halloween. He tries to cut out the spider's body but his first effort ends in disaster when the scissors slip and he cuts the body in half. His second and third efforts are no better and he is frustrated with the 'stupid scissors'. Maura, his key worker, shows him how to hold the scissors so they won't slip; she then demonstrates how to cut out the spider's body. Alex's fourth attempt is successful and with Maura's help he sticks on each of the eight fuzzy felt spider legs.

Support for Vygotsky's ZPD theory is provided in a number of studies, including Freund's seminal doll's house experiment. As part of her doctoral research, Freund (1990) explored mother–child interactions using two groups of children aged between 3 and 5 years. The task involved selecting and placing items of furniture in a doll's house. The first group of children completed a similar task with help from their mother (ZPD) before working on the experimental task alone. The second group had no previous guidance and worked alone on the task (Piaget's discovery learning). Freund found that children with prior experience and support from their mothers easily completed the task, whereas the second group were less proficient. She concluded that guided learning within the ZPD led to greater understanding/performance than working alone (discovery learning).

Effective scaffolding appears to have a number of general features which Applebee and Langer (1983, cited in Zhao and Orey, 1999, p. 6) summarized as including:

1 **Intentionality**: The task has a clear overall purpose driving any separate activity that may contribute to the whole.
2 **Appropriateness**: Instructional tasks pose problems that can be solved with help but which students cannot successfully complete on their own.
3 **Structure**: Modelling and questioning activities are structured around a model of appropriate approaches to the task and lead to a natural sequence of thought and language.
4 **Collaboration**: The teacher's response to student work recasts and expands upon the students' efforts without rejecting what they have accomplished on their own. The teacher's primary role is collaborative rather than evaluative.
5 **Internalization**: External scaffolding for the activity is gradually withdrawn as the patterns are internalized by the students.

Vygotsky believed that children create their own ZPD during play. He believed that 'play creates a zone of proximal development for the child. In play a child always behaves beyond his average age, above his daily behaviour' (1987, p. 102, cited in Hogan and Tudge, 1999). Although he cautioned against an over intellectualizing of children's play, he believed it was highly important in young children's development, particularly in the use of symbolic forms.

PEER COLLABORATION

The subject of peer collaboration was discussed at length in Chapter 4 where Piaget's views on peer collaboration are explored. For a full understanding of the advantages and disadvantages of peer collaboration, it is important that you refer back to that section. One of the main tenets of Piaget's theory was the belief that peer interaction was effective when one member of the dyad had achieved an understanding of conservation. Drawing on evidence from his own research, he concluded that non-conservers were more likely to attain conservation through their experience of working with a more expert peer than when working alone. Similarly, Vygotsky believed that collaboration was more effective when one member of the dyad had greater experience than the other. Whereas Piaget discussed peer interaction, Vygotsky focused on adult-led interactions, particularly between the teacher and the child. Two key concepts underpin Vygotsky's theory. The first is the zone of proximal development previously discussed in this chapter. The second concerns the concept of intersubjectivity which seeks to bring different perspectives together to form an agreed view. For example, Josh (aged 3 years and 3 months) is playing with his garage but the lift bringing the cars from the bottom to the top level isn't working. His dad has a look and asks him what the problem is; Josh explains that 'it's broken'. On examination, his dad finds a crayon lodged in the mechanism. Following his dad's instructions, Josh removes the crayon. Once free, the lift works again. Here, Josh and his father start from different perspectives but working collaboratively come to a mutual or intersubjective understanding.

According to Vygotsky:

> he continues to work in collaboration even though the teacher is not standing near him ... This help – this aspect of collaboration – is invisibly present. It is contained in what looks from the outside like the child's independent solution of the problems. (1987–1998, p. 216)

A central theme of Piaget and Vygotsky's theory is the effectiveness of asymmetric relationships which foster the transfer of knowledge from a more knowledgeable peer to a less experienced learner. Both theorists believed that asymmetric relationship which includes peers who bring the same knowledge to a problem is no different from the child solving the problem alone. Similar to Piaget, Vygotsky was more concerned with the process than the product of higher order thinking. For that reason, he tended to focus on the social interaction taking place during collaborative learning rather than on the benefit of the experience for the learner. Although much of the research on collaborative learning reports positive benefits (see Chapter 4 for a discussion), there are discrepancies about the conditions which mediate improvement (Hogan and Tudge, 1999). Factors which can impact upon the effectiveness of peer collaboration include the children's age, their ability level, their motivation to succeed, the nature of the task and contextual or cultural support for collaboration.

Another problem in collaborative relationships concerns the issue of ownership and the importance afforded each participant's perspective. For example, Jacob (aged 3 years and 5 months) is building a tower with bricks. He searches for smaller bricks to place at the top of his tower but each brick he selects is too large or too small and falls off. His brother Moses (aged 6 years and 7 months) decides to help. He points to the yellow angled bricks and asks Jacob to hand him one, then another and another. As Moses successfully places each brick in position, Jacob becomes increasingly agitated. Eventually he points at Moses and tells him to 'go away. They's mine bricks, not youse bricks'. In attempting to help Jacob, Moses took control of the problem rendering Jacob's efforts redundant. According to

Tudge (1992), children can and do support each other's thinking but there are times when peer collaboration can have an adverse effect upon one or both members of the dyad.

CRITICISMS OF VYGOTSKY

A number of criticisms have been levelled at the interpretation of Vygotsky's work. For example, it is argued that Vygotsky did not describe himself as a social constructivist; this label was attached by contemporary scholars during the translation of his work (Hua Liu and Matthews, 2005). Translations of his work from Russian into English have led to an emphasis on some aspects of his work to the detriment of others and to superficial interpretations. By way of example, the ZPD thought to exemplify Vygotsky's theory appears less than nine times in all of the thousands of pages he wrote (Kamen and Murphy, 2012). It is also argued that, in keeping with his Marxist ideology, Vygotsky was concerned with society and people at the collective rather than the individual level (Resnick, 1996). Implicit in Vygotsky's theory is the rather optimistic notion that all social and cultural experiences will have a positive impact upon the developing child. Yet the cases of Victoria Climbé and Baby P remind us that some children live and die in appalling circumstances.

Vygotsky's emphasis on the importance of language in the development of learning has been roundly criticized by Fox (2001) who points out that if thought cannot exist without language, until a child begins to speak they must be devoid of thought. He continues by arguing that this theory 'ignores all the implicit knowledge we have of the world which we have never put into words' (2001: 29–30).

According to Daniels (2005), many of Vygotsky's theories are incomplete and lack sophistication. This may be attributed to his early death at the age of 38 and the fact that his understanding of psychology and psychological theories was derived from personal study when his university training was in the artsand theatre.

VYGOTSKY IN ACTION: GOLDEN KEY SCHOOLS

Definition

Perestroika: The policy of reconstructing a series of political and economic reforms in the former Soviet Union under the leadership of Mikhail Gorbachov which encouraged trade between Russia and non-Marxist countries.

Led by Elena Kravtsova (Vygotsky's granddaughter), since 1989 and with Perestroika over, 30 Golden Key Schools have been established to develop Vygotsky's socio-cultural theory of education. Kamen and Murphy (2012, p. 4) detail how the Golden Key programme developed from a number of programmes and educational philosophies including: Swedish kindergartens, the English nurturing system, Steiner's anthroposophy, Waldorf's pedagogy and the seminal work of Vygotsky. Reflecting the core principles of socio-cultural theory, Golden Key Schools are premised on the promotion of culture and history. Catering for children between 3 and 10 years of age, Robbins (2010) and Kamen and Murphy (2012) describe the five principles in the programme as follows:

1 **Mixed age groups**: The school has mixed-age and single-age teaching to allow the older children to reflect their learning on to younger children, who benefit from learning from more advanced peers.
2 **Family principles**: Golden Key Schools are organized around family principles, including active parental involvement. Children are taught in 'families' of 15 to 25 children aged between 3 and 10 years of age rather than in classes. The children meet in their families every school day to discuss problems and to learn to solve problems. Since there are children of different ages in each family, the older children model behaviour and support the younger children.
3 **Meaningful events or happenings**: Lessons are centred on events which are highly meaningful to the child and touch their emotions. Subsequently, each lesson follows a plot directly related to the event.
4 **Interaction and interdependence**: The focus is on the interaction and interdependence of education and development. This ensures that lessons are age-appropriate and that learning takes place within the ZPD.
5 **Paired pedagogues**: Classes are taught by two teachers, one acting as expert and the other as a novice, who asks questions to extend the children's knowledge and understanding.

Similarities can be drawn between the Vygotskian philosophy that frames Golden Key Schools and Reggio Emilia. Similar to Golden Key Schools, the teacher in the internationally renowned schools in Reggio Emilia, Italy, play a central role in helping children plan and execute their work. They guide discussions and activities and monitor outcomes. Reflecting the central tenet of Vygotsky's theory, teachers in Reggio schools scaffold learning and provide stimulating environments to promote discussions and challenge children's thinking (O'Brien, 2002). Both approaches seek to develop children who are securely embedded within their social and cultural group.

Vygotsky's influence is not confined to Russia. He continues to have a presence in early years settings in many countries in the developed world. This is particularly evident in recent educational reforms in the UK (Desirable Outcomes for Children's Learning on Entering Compulsory Education [SCAA, 1996]; Early Learning Goals [QCA, 2000]; The National Strategies Early Years document (DE, 2010)), predicated on the notion that instruction can and should precede learning. Similarly, his theory has had a significant impact on the development of a new school of thought, variously termed the new social studies of childhood and the new sociology of childhood, discussed in Chapter 8.

Summary

Like Piaget, Vygotsky believed that young children are curious and actively involved in their own learning and the discovery and development of new understandings/schema. Vygotsky's pedagogical theory is based on the Marxist view of relations between human consciousness and the material world. He believed that children develop in a social matrix formed by the interconnection of social relationships and interactions between themselves and other children. These experiences are internalized as thought. One of his most controversial claims concerns the notion that thought is internalized language. Interpreted literally, this theory implies that a child with a language delay or language difficulty is either only partially able to think or devoid of thought.

Whereas Piaget emphasized self-initiated discovery, Vygotsky focused on the role of the teacher. He did not believe that children were passive recipients of knowledge informed by knowledgeable teachers but viewed the teacher as a facilitator of learning. The social environment is given prominence in teaching, with effective teachers providing a stimulating and challenging learning environment. Reminiscent of Piaget's theory about assimilation and accommodation, Vygotsky believed that new knowledge builds on and extends previous knowledge. Through sensitive teaching and peer collaboration, a child can walk a 'head taller'. The ZPD is perhaps the most widely referenced aspect of Vygotsky's work. Through observation or testing, an early years practitioner begins by determining the child's existing level of knowledge and, through skilful mentoring, extends the child's learning. He termed the difference between the child's existing knowledge base and higher level thinking the ZPD. The issue of understood learning was developed by a group of American researchers who sought to understand how learning and thinking can be scaffolded through the ZPD metaphor. Scaffolding is discussed in greater detail in Chapter 6. Although criticisms have been levelled against Vygotsky's work, they mostly concern the incomplete nature of his work. Nevertheless, for many, he remains 'The Mozart of Psychology'.

Table 5.1 The strengths and weaknesses of Vygotsky's theory

Strengths	Weaknesses
Adopts a child-centred approach. Children are viewed as active and powerful participants in the learning process.	
Emphasizes the role of culture and the environment in the child's learning.	
Offers a theory of cognitive development. Roughly associated with age, Vygotsky did not believe that development followed a fixed stage and invariant approach. On the contrary, he believed that a difficult task may cause a child to revert to earlier forms of learning such as counting on their fingers.	Many early years theorists dispute suggestions of staged development, arguing it fails to take account of individual differences.
Employs qualitative approaches including observations and listening to children as they completed tasks.	1 He conducted very few studies to support his claims. 2 Supporting evidence for his claims is supplied by his supporters who interpreted his meaning.
Is based on a belief that learning can precede understanding. Children can be taught concepts that extend and develop their current learning.	
Focuses on process rather than product.	
Recognizes the central importance of play.	
Is based on a belief that language precedes thought.	This is a highly controversial claim. Children without speech or who have limited speech, according to this notion, would be incapable of thought.
Explains the internalization of language as thought.	
Identifies the importance of peer interaction and collaborative learning.	
Affords the teacher a central role in the child's learning. Teachers are considered facilitators who scaffold and develop learning.	
Identifies the importance of developing the child's potential.	The zone of proximal development is frequently misunderstood and given greater prominence by academics and students than afforded by Vygotsky. The theory has been translated and truncated to exclude Vygotsky's Marxist views. Translations have led to misinterpretations.

Table 5.2   Similarities in Vygotsky and Piaget's theoretical perspectives

Child centred: They both adopted a child-centred approach. Children are viewed as active and powerful participants in the learning process.

Cognitive conflict: They both believed that cognitive development is initiated by cognitive conflict. Piaget termed the state of cognitive imbalance which drives learning 'disequilibration'.

Constructivism: They were both constructivists and believed that cognition is the result of mental construction. A constructivist teacher creates a context for learning in which students can become engaged in interesting activities that encourage and facilitate learning.

Experiential learning: They both believed that intelligence comes from actions. Experiential learning experiences might involve the child in baking cookies, growing watercress, playing games or creating using junk art. Through these activities, the child constructs knowledge.

Peer collaboration: They both identified the importance of peer interaction and collaborative learning. They believed that effective peer collaboration was asymmetric to foster the transfer of knowledge from a more knowledgeable peer to a less experienced learner.

Process: They both focused on the process of learning rather than on the product. They were more concerned with how a child arrived at their solution to a problem than the answer.

Social environment: They both believed that interaction with the physical and social environment is critical for cognitive growth. Visits to the local fire station, park, theatre or seaside will extend the young child's social learning experiences.

Qualitative methods: They both employed qualitative approaches, including observations of children, as they completed tasks and interviews with children.

RECOMMENDED READING

Daniels, H. (ed.) (2005) *An Introduction to Vygotsky*, 2nd edn. London: Routledge Taylor & Francis.

This is a must read for students who hope to grapple with the complexity of Vygotsky's theory. It is not an easy read and will challenge students. Nevertheless, it remains one of the most thorough texts of its type.

Smidt, S. (2009). *Introducing Vygotsky: A Guide for Practitioners and Students in Early Years Education.* London: Routledge.

This useful resource offers a discussion of Vygotskian theory with examples included to ensure understanding. Definitions are provided throughout the text to explain some of the more esoteric terms employed.

REFERENCES

Benson, B. (1997). Scaffolding (coming to terms). *English Journal, 86, 7,* 126–27.
Bruner, J.S. (1986). *Actual Minds, Possible Worlds.* Cambridge, MA: Harvard University Press.
Corsaro, W.A. (1992). Interpretative reproduction in children's peer cultures. *Social Psychology Quarterly, 55,* 160–77.

Daniels, H. (ed.) (2005). *An Introduction to Vygotsky*, 2nd edn. London: Routledge Taylor & Francis.

Department of Education (DE) (2010). *The National Strategies Early Years Document*. Available at: www.education.gov.uk/schools/toolsandinitiatives/nationalstrategies

Fox, R. (2001). Constructivism examined. *Oxford Review of Education, 27, 1*, 23–35.

Freund, L.S. (1990). Maternal regulation of children's problem-solving behavior and its impact on children's performance. *Child Development, 61, 1*, 113–26.

Hogan, D.M. & Tudge, J.R.H. (1999). Implications of Vygotsky's theory for peer learning. In A.M. O'Donnell & A. King (eds) *Cognitive Perspectives on Peer Learning* Mahwah, NJ: Lawrence Erlbaum. pp. 39–66.

Holzman, L. (2006). Activating postmodernism. *Theory and Psychology, 16, 1*, 109–23.

Hua Liu, C. & Matthews, R. (2005). Vygotsky's philosophy: constructivism and its criticisms examined. *International Educational Journal, 6, 3*, 386–99.

Kamen, M. & Murphy, C. (2012 forthcoming). Science education at the Golden Key Schools: learning science in Vygotskian-based elementary schools in Russia. In D.F. Berline & A.L. White (eds) *International Consortium for Research in Science and Mathematics Education.* Columbus, CH: Ohio State University.

Meadows, S. (1993). *The Child as Thinker: The Development and Acquisition of Cognition in Childhood.* London: Routledge.

Murphy, C. (2012 forthcoming). Vygotsky and primary science. In *Second International Handbook of Science Education.* New York: Springer. Chapter 2.6.

O'Brien, L.M. (2002). *A Response to Dewey and Vygotsky: Society, Experience, and Inquiry in Educational Practice.* Washington, DC: AERA.

Pagram, J. & McMahon, M. (1997). WeB-CD: An Interactive Learning Experience for Distance Education Students Studying Interactive Multimedia. Poster presented at ICCE97 International Conference on Computers in Education, Kuching, Malaysia, 2–6 December.

Palinscar, A.S. (1998). Social constructivist perspectives on teaching and learning. *Annual Review of Pyschology, 49, 1*, 345–75.

Pea, R.D. (1993). Practices of distributed intelligence and designs for education. In G. Salomon (ed.) *Distributed Cognitions* (pp. 47–87). New York: Cambridge University Press.

Qualifications and Curriculum Authority (QCA) (2000). *Early Learning Goals.* London: QCA.

Resnick, L.B. (1996). Situated learning. In E. De Corte & F.E. Weinert (eds) *International Encyclopedia of Developmental and Instructional Psychology* (pp. 341–7). Oxford: Elsevier.

Robbins, D. (2010). *Golden Key Schools.* Available at: http://faculty.ucmo.edu/drobbins/html/golden_key_schools.html (accessed 16 June 2011).

Rose, S.A., Feldman, J.F. & Jankowski, J.J. (2003). The building blocks of cognition. *The Journal of Pediatrics, 143, 4*, 54–61.

Schaffer, H.R. (2004). *Introducing Child Psychology.* Oxford: Blackwell.

School Curriculum Assessment Authority (SCAA) (1996). *Nursery Education: Desirable Outcomes for Children's Learning on Entering Compulsory Education.* London: SCAA and Department for Education and Employment. ED 433 091.

Smidt, S. (2009). *Introducing Vygotsky: A Guide for Practitioners and Students in Early Years Education.* London: Routledge.

Sutherland, P. (1992). *Cognitive Development Today: Piaget and his Critics.* London: Paul Chapman Publishing.

Toulmin, S. (1978). The Mozart of Psychology. *New York Review of Books, 28:* 51–7.

Tudge, J.R.H. (1992). Processes and consequences of peer collaboration. *Child Development, 63,* 1364–79.

Tudge, J.R.H. & Winterhoff, P.A. (1993). Vygotsky, Piaget, and Bandura: perspectives on the relations between the social world and cognitive development. *Human Development, 36,* 61–81.

Vygotsky, L.S. (1956). *Selected Psychological Investigations.* Moscow: Izdatel'stvoAcademii Pedagogicheskikh Nauk.

Vygotsky, L.S. (1962). *Thought and Language.* Cambridge, MA: MIT.

Vygotsky, L.S. (1978). *Mind in Society: The Development of Higher Psychological Processes.* Cambridge, MA: Harvard University Press.

Vygotsky, L.S. (1981). The development of higher forms of attention in childhood. In J.V. Wertsch (ed.) *The Concept of Activity in Soviet Psychology.* Armonk, NY: Sharpe.

Vygotsky, L.S. (1983). Istorija razvitija vystchych psykhicheskych functsyj. In *Vygotsky, L.S., Collected Works in 6 Volumes.* Vol 3. Moscow: Pedagogica.

Vygotsky, L.S. (1987–1998). *The Collected Works of L.S. Vygotsky. Volume I: Problems of General Psychology. Volume II: The Fundamentals of Defectology. Volume III: Problems of the Theory and History of Psychology. Volume IV: The History of Development of Higher Mental Functions. Volume V: Child Psychology.* (Editor of the English translation: R.W. Rieber.) New York: Plenum Press.

Wertsch, J.V. (ed) (1981). *The Concept of Activity in Soviet Psychology.* Armonk, NY: M.E. Sharpe.

Wood, D., Bruner, J.S. & Ross, G.R. (1976). The role of tutoring in problem-solving. *Journal of Child Psychology and Psychiatry, 17, 2,* 89–100.

Wood, E. (2011). Progression and Challenge in Play from 5–11. Inaugural lecture, Stranmillis University College, a College of The Queen's University of Belfast, 15 June.

Zhao, R. & Orey, M. (1999). *The Scaffolding Process: Concepts, Features, and Empirical Studies.* Unpublished manuscript, University of Georgia.

6 BANDURA, BRONFENBRENNER AND SOCIAL LEARNING

This chapter aims to:

- explore the work of Albert Bandura and how it contributes to our understanding of social learning
- examine the work of Urie Bronfenbrenner in relation to that of Bandura
- explore how Bandura and Bronfenbrenner's theoretical perspectives can help our understanding of children's learning and social development.

INTRODUCTION

This chapter explores the work of two influential theorists who have attempted to explain the nature of social learning. It begins with the work of Albert Bandura before drawing upon the more recent views of Urie Bronfenbrenner. Bandura believed that social factors were central to the learning and development of the individual and, in the 1970s, he introduced his *social learning theory* (Bandura, 1977). In doing so, he moved significantly from some of his contemporaries who espoused a more purely behaviourist approach. For Bandura, learning did not always involve changes in behaviour and children could, for example, observe others without their observations necessarily leading to a change in their own behaviour. Unlike the early behaviourists, he suggested that motivation played a significant role in the link between children observing behaviours and subsequent changes in their own behaviour. Bandura saw motivation, therefore, as a key factor in the development and learning of young children.

Bronfenbrenner's theory differs from that of Bandura in a number of ways. In particular, he viewed factors in the child's wider social, political and economic environment as being of much greater importance than Bandura and other theorists working in the field of child development. Unlike Bandura, Bronfenbrenner's theory has at its core the view that a child's own biology is a key factor influencing their development. His theory, therefore, can be best understood as the interrelationship of children with the environments in which they live.

A question that continues to exercise many professionals is why so many children in modern societies succeed when so many others fail. Why, despite years of formal education, do significant numbers of children fail to develop their potential and live lives characterized by lack of ambition, low self-esteem and disaffection whilst others gain material success and status and develop confidence in their own abilities? What factors in their early years cause one child's life to differ so much from another's? The newspaper columnist James Chapman, writing in a British newspaper, The *Daily Mail* (18 April 2011), recently commented:

> Some 46 per cent of children are born to unmarried mothers, according to research by the Centre for Social Justice. The think-tank said a child growing up in a one-parent family is 75 per cent more likely to fail at school, 70 per cent more likely to become a drug addict, 50 per cent more likely to have an alcohol problem and 35 per cent more likely to be unemployed as an adult. (p. 6)

Such stark statistics need to be treated with considerable caution. Many children grow up in lone-parent families and are happy and successful. However, such newspaper articles do reflect a concern amongst some that many young children are failing to have access to important life chances that will enable them, as they grow older, to develop their potential (Buckingham, 2000). The following two cases present a number of issues common to many children and offer a focus for understanding the work of Bandura and Bronfenbrenner. Compare the examples below.

Example

1 Tracey, aged 6, is described by her teacher as, 'a lively little girl who can try very hard'. She lives with her mother and two older step-brothers. Tracey's mother has just begun a relationship with a man she met recently. He is aggressive and verbally abusive and both she and her brother Matthew, aged 3, become frightened when he gets angry. Matthew attends playgroup and is beginning to imitate the aggressive behaviours of his mother's new partner. Tracey's mother is unemployed. Tracey's recent school report described her reading as very poor and noted that she could not say the alphabet in sequence. Tracey is also described by her teacher as, 'not good at forming friendships' and as 'always seeking attention from the Learning Support Assistant'. When assessed by an educational psychologist following concerns about progress and occasional aggressive behaviour, she recorded low scores on vocabulary and verbal comprehension tests. Of note, however, were Tracey's abilities in areas of reasoning, which fell within the superior range, suggesting that she was very able but with specific learning difficulties compounded by delayed

language development, impoverished vocabulary and poorly developed strategies for sustaining attention.

2   Ben, aged 6, is described by his teacher as 'articulate, socially skilled and exceptionally bright'. He lives at home with his parents, two older brothers and Gemma, his sister, who is aged 2. Both his parents have benefited from university education and hold professional positions where they earn well and have a wide circle of friends, all of whom work as highly paid professionals. Ben's parents are patient with him and take time to explain to him why they become upset when he behaves in ways that they disapprove of. Though only 6 years of age, Ben has already travelled widely and is used to being in the company of successful, motivated and articulate adults. Ben was able to read simple books at the end of his first year of schooling and his reading and spelling ages are currently well in advance of his chronological age – his reading age was recently measured as 8 years and 6 months, and his spelling age as 7 years and 6 months. His vocabulary is considered by his teacher to be 'very advanced'. Ben is sociable and has many friendship groups.

Our understanding of Tracey and Ben's learning, and their social and emotional development, can be greatly enhanced by drawing upon the theoretical perspectives offered by Bandura and Bronfenbrenner. First, however, it is important to examine the key elements of Bandura's social learning theory.

ALBERT BANDURA

Albert Bandura (born 1925)

Albert Bandura was born in 1925 in Canada and is perhaps best known for his *social learning theory*, and the Bobo doll experiment conducted in 1961. In this experiment, Bandura filmed a woman aggressively hitting a large toy doll known as a Bobo doll. Bandura then showed this film to a group of young children who were given the opportunity to play in a separate room which contained a Bobo doll. These children then began to hit the doll as they had observed the woman doing. In this regard, they were imitating the aggressive behaviour of the woman. Of interest was the fact that the children were not being rewarded for hitting the doll. They were in fact engaging in behaviours they had observed but that had not been reinforced. Learning was, therefore, taking place, not as behaviourists of the time would have argued, as a result of reinforcement, but as a result of observation. Bandura believed that the stimulus–response explanation of learning proposed by the early behaviourists was overly simplistic and did not go far enough in explaining human behaviour and emotions.

Whilst Bandura acknowledged that classical and operant conditioning (see Chapter 3) could go some way in explaining social learning, he also argued that there were two other factors that were of great importance, namely *imitation* and *identification*.

Bandura suggested that both of these factors provided for accelerated social learning in children. With the first of these, children imitate the behaviours of others whilst, with the second, new learning is assimilated into existing concepts that have already been internalized by the child. In this way, Bandura argued, whole patterns of behaving become internalized by children such that they then act upon new situations in the way they think that the adults from whom they have modelled their behaviour would behave. In the case of Tracey and Ben, they have internalized quite different patterns of behaviour that have been modelled by the adults in their families and by significant others they have come into contact with during those crucial pre-school years, and their first years of schooling. Tracey's younger brother Matthew will also have learned from observing the behaviours that Tracey models, which may be characterized at times by anxiety and anger. On the other hand, Gemma, Ben's younger sister, will have observed Ben as being confident and enthusiastic and socially skilled. She will also have benefited from listening to Ben's more sophisticated use of language and from observing non-verbal communication such as his mannerisms and listening skills that he employs when he presents himself in social situations. In this way, her social learning is very different to that of Matthew.

Of course, it was recognized by Bandura that for positive and meaningful learning to take place, the behaviours of those adults being imitated by children need to be appropriate. Take the case of Tracey's younger brother, Matthew, who regularly witnesses his mother's partner being physically and verbally aggressive towards his mother. When Matthew observes arguments between his mother and her new partner, he often feels that he is to blame and that their arguments are due to his own behaviours. He may well even come to internalize a perception of himself as being a 'bad' child. This is unlikely to happen in the case of Gemma, Ben's younger sister, who will almost certainly come to internalize a view of herself as being capable and successful, and loved, as she observes the behaviours of others around her as being wholly appropriate, positive and purposeful. Unlike Matthew, Gemma is almost certain to receive regular positive feedback from her parents and older brothers, which will serve to reinforce those behaviours that her parents desire of her such as attentiveness, confidence and independence. In this way, these aspects of her personality and the manner in which she presents herself in social situations will have been imitated and identified with – in other words, they have become learned. Here, we can make reference to the approaches found in Steiner Waldorf settings. Miller and Pound have commented:

> Steiner practitioners observe that young children are nurtured by the security of rhythm and repetition – within which their inherent skills and abilities can flourish … Having well thought through and repeated routines builds habits that are useful (properly washed hands), respectful (creating a peaceful mood at the table) and comforting ('this is how we always do it here'). (2011, p. 92)

Whilst Tracey and Matthew, unlike Ben and Gemma, fail to have the security of rhythm and repetition in their home life, where most of their everyday experiences are characterized by chaos and inconsistency with, for example, irregular meals and bedtimes, they can, however, gain from feelings of security and nurturing in their primary school and playgroup, respectively.

According to Bandura's social learning theory, Matthew may come to imitate the aggressive behaviours of his mother's new partner and these may, in turn, be played out at his playgroup when he is with other children. It is possible that Matthew will identify with his mother's partner and may come to be viewed by others at his playgroup as an aggressive child, and he may start to live up to this perception by others. Bandura's social learning theory would suggest that Matthew is beginning to acquire a type of exterior, which has been learned through observing and imitating the behaviours of his mother's partner. Such was the case with the young children in the Bobo doll experiment referred to earlier, which Bandura used to emphasize how young children will observe and imitate the behaviours of others. It is an interesting, and worrying, aspect of human social and emotional development that individuals may, in stressful situations, 'identify with the aggressor' simply as a means of defending themselves.

Bandura suggested that children not only observe physical behaviours but that they also observe the verbal behaviours of others, which includes expectations that others make of them (Linden, 2005). He suggested that young children observe adults as they offer verbal narratives and descriptions of events and as they use language and gesture to communicate their ideas, thoughts, instructions, questions, and so on. Given that Ben is frequently in the company of articulate and successful adults, it is certain that he will learn many positive aspects of behaving and interacting with others through observing their behaviours, as well as the responses they receive, which invariably will be characterized by the attentive and interested responses of others. It is worth noting that Bandura also proposed a type of symbolic modelling where children engage in imitation and identification of individuals who are not real but fictional, such as the type of characters found in fairy tales and children's stories. The ever-increasing number of visual stories and cartoons found in children's television, the cinema and computer games can be included within this type of symbolic modelling.

A further key element of Bandura's theory, which is directly relevant to practitioners working with young children, is that of self-efficacy (Bandura, 1997). Having a better knowledge and understanding of self-efficacy is very important for professionals working with young children in educational and care settings. Bandura saw self-efficacy as a child's belief in their abilities to do well and to succeed in certain situations, and as their capacity to exercise control over their own actions in order to gain success. He proposed that self-efficacy is directly related to how children think and act, as well as to their emotional state. In effect, Bandura has influenced the way in which we try to understand the goals that individuals – be they children, parents or professionals – aim to achieve. Children with poor self-efficacy, for example, have a tendency to avoid tasks that present them with a challenge, preferring instead to focus on the negative and frame their thinking within constructs whereby they come to convince themselves that they cannot achieve. Children with poor self-efficacy typically present themselves in social situations as having low self-confidence.

Directly linked to a child's capacity to gain success are the child's feelings about themselves and others, and the world around them. In recent years, there has been a resurgence of interest amongst psychologists and educators regarding self-efficacy, and particularly an increased recognition of how a child's self-efficacy influences and affects their learning and behaviour. Faced with having to organize their own time and with identifying learning goals and targets, children with poor self-efficacy will typically do less well than those with strong self-efficacy. They may, for example, demonstrate little interest in attempting tasks and seeing them through to completion and may feel less committed to working with their peers. They may also demonstrate greater signs of anxiety than their peers when asked to engage in problem-based learning tasks. Colverd and Hodgkin have stressed how children in learning situations may:

> place limits on what they think is possible, believing a task is beyond their capability. Lack of self-belief affects their motivation and their commitment to learning. 'I can't do this, it's boring' signals 'I don't believe I can be successful with this and therefore I don't want to take the risk – it may or may not be boring'. (2011, p. 36)

Bandura believed that a key factor in developing a strong sense of self-efficacy was the development of 'mastery' through experiences, for example in observing others who are succeeding, having positive and affirming comments from others, and understanding one's own emotions and feelings. Self-efficacy as an integral part of a child's early learning experiences, therefore, has enormous implications for practitioners working with children in early years settings and primary schools.

Exercise

Identify occasions when you have observed children displaying 'good' self-efficacy. Consider how this has developed within the children and what factors might have influenced this process. Consider how modelling might have influenced the development of self-efficacy in these cases.

In order to understand social learning more fully as well as the impact upon children of their wider social environments, it is helpful to look more closely at learning within the wider social, political and economic contexts within which children grow up. Whilst Bandura's work tended to focus on the individual, other theorists have focused more upon more extraneous factors. One particular theoretical perspective that goes much further in exploring these wider contexts is that offered by Urie Bronfenbrenner. Bronfenbrenner's work offers a further dimension to that of Bandura's and provides the means for much greater critical reflection and understanding of how young children learn, and the cultural contexts and factors that influence the course of their development from early childhood through adolescence and into adulthood.

URIE BRONFENBRENNER

Bronfenbrenner (born 1917)

Bronfenbrenner was born in Moscow and when he was 6 years of age he moved with his family to the USA. Bronfenbrenner gained a scholarship to Cornell University in 1934 where he studied psychology. He subsequently served in the army from 1942 to 1946 in the latter years of the Second World War working as a psychologist. In 1979, Bronfenbrenner published a seminal text, *The Ecology of Human Development*, in which he set out his views on child development. Bronfenbrenner was co-founder of the Head Start programme and is perhaps best known for his *Ecological Systems Model*, now redefined as the *Bioecological Model*.

Bronfenbrenner emphasized how children grow up in constantly changing and dynamic cultures in which they must interact with and relate to those around them in ever-shifting contexts (Bronfenbrenner, 1979; Bronfenbrenner and Ceci, 1994). As children grow and develop, the nature and quality of their interactions change and this process occurs within communities, cultures and wider societies, all of which have their own definable and recognizable characteristics (Johnston and Nahmad-Williams, 2009). Bronfenbrenner 'emphasizes the importance of studying "development-in-context", or the ecology of development' (Smith et al., 2003, p. 9). Take, for example, the cases of Tracey and Ben – consider that they are now older and in their first year of secondary school. Here, it is important to emphasize how early years practitioners need to think ahead and see the children they work with not only as 'early years' children but as unique individuals who are in the beginning stages of the rest of their lives.

Example

Some years have passed and Tracey and Ben are now in their first year of secondary school where there are relatively high levels of disaffection amongst a small number of the older pupils, but high levels of achievement and aspiration amongst the majority of pupils who are aiming to move into the school's sixth form and then on to third-level education. Tracey's mother has become more settled in her life and has gained employment. Her previous partner has left the family home and a new partner has moved in. Though he is not aggressive, he is unemployed and has been for over 10 years. Ben's life has changed dramatically in that his mother has died. Money has become an issue and his father has had to take on extra part-time work in order to look after the family. Despite these challenges Ben continues to be highly motivated and focused and is developing some positive friendships with like-minded pupils in his year who are also focused and motivated. Following transfer to her secondary school, Tracey has become increasingly influenced by her new peer group, which consists mainly of children who have experienced problems in their primary schools relating to behaviour and lack of progress. She appears to be more drawn to the older pupils who are disaffected and during break times observes them closely.

Not only is the physical and geographical context of Tracey and Ben's new school very different to their primary school, the culture of their new school environment is also fundamentally distinctive with new rules to be learned, new expectations exercised by teachers, and more particularly, a whole new set of expectations from their peers. Differences in fashion are more pronounced in their new school and they have to start absorbing and understanding the hidden rules and behaviours of their peers and especially the older teenage boys and girls. In addition to these more immediate factors, society and its legal structure recognizes that Tracey and Ben are now older and as such they will increasingly have expectations placed upon them to act and behave with much greater responsibility and accountability. The other children in the school, and particularly the older children, will act as role models for Tracey and Ben. It will be Tracey and Ben's early upbringing and the modelling of their own parents, and the relationships they had in their early years with significant others, that will now serve to give them stability and support them in resisting being drawn into potentially problematic social situations and maintaining a focus and good motivation in their new educational setting.

Whilst Bronfenbrenner placed significant emphasis upon the wider environment when attempting to explore child development, he also proposed that it is important to think of a number of layers that encompass children as they develop. These layers, both directly and indirectly, affect the biological maturation of every child. Bronfenbrenner's theory, therefore, requires that in order to fully explore child development, we need also to take into account the wider environmental influences upon the child. The layers that define Bronfenbrenner's theory are sometimes likened to Russian dolls, where smaller dolls are placed within much bigger ones (Linden, 2005). Bronfenbrenner gave a name to each of the layers that surrounded the child. The closest and most immediate layer to the child is the 'Microsystem'.

Definitions

Microsystem: Immediate environments (family, school, peer group, neighbourhood and childcare environments).

Mesosystem: A system comprised of connections between immediate environments (i.e. a child's home and school).

Exosystem: External environmental settings which only indirectly affect development (such as a parent's workplace).

Macrosystem: The larger cultural context (Eastern vs Western culture, national economy, political culture, subculture).

Chronosystem: The patterning of environmental events and transitions over the course of life.

It is within the Microsystem that the child has their most direct contact with, for example, their family, their nursery school or playgroup, their community and their neighbours. Bronfenbrenner proposed a two-way process within this layer that influenced the child, referring to these as 'bi-directional influences'. Whilst the child is influenced by the behaviours, actions and beliefs of their parents, the child in turn also influences the parents. Take the example of an infant in the cot who suddenly and for no apparent reason makes a joyful cooing noise. When the mother hears the noise, she comes running from the other room and lifts the child and gives lots of warm, nurturing hugs. In this situation, the child has initiated the interaction and the mother has responded. As such, the infant is in fact influencing the mother's behaviour. As Bronfenbrenner would suggest, the relation is bi-directional. Bronfenbrenner has suggested that these bi-directional influences are very strong.

The next layer outside of the 'Microsystem' is the 'Mesosystem', which relates to the construction of connections between, for example, the child's mother and father and their first teacher, or between their local community and their school. Here, the child relates experiences gained in school to those gained in their family. The child is, therefore, drawing comparisons between their teachers and their parents, between their new school friends, and friends in their neighbourhood, and between the wider family such as between brothers and sisters, and cousins. If the child's

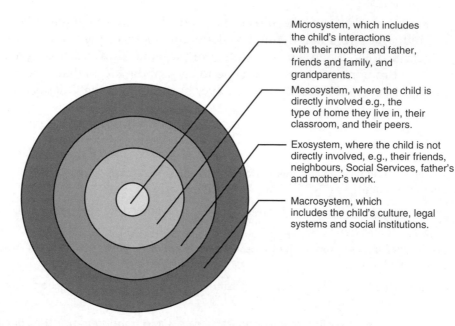

Microsystem, which includes the child's interactions with their mother and father, friends and family, and grandparents.

Mesosystem, where the child is directly involved e.g., the type of home they live in, their classroom, and their peers.

Exosystem, where the child is not directly involved, e.g., their friends, neighbours, Social Services, father's and mother's work.

Macrosystem, which includes the child's culture, legal systems and social institutions.

Figure 6.1   Bronfenbrenner's Ecological Model of individual development

family members are regular and frequent members of a sports club, for example, then there will be connections and comparisons made between those individuals within the club and their lifestyles and their own family context.

Outside of the 'Mesosystem' lies the 'Exosystem' – the child's wider social system. Here, for example, the work commitments of parents, or their levels of income, impact upon the child's Microsystem. Within the Exosystem the wider social experiences of children will also impact indirectly upon them. An example is the current economic climate in the UK where it is proposed that many public libraries will be closed and that the Forestry Commission will sell a percentage of its forested land to private developers, thus promoting fears amongst many that important resources and activities will become lost to many children, young people and their families. A further example can be seen in the UK where the new coalition government in 2011 is proposing to introduce significant changes to schooling through the introduction of 'free schools', much greater choice for parents, and a restructuring of the way in which teachers are trained. All of these external factors will exert significant influence upon the lives of many children in the UK.

Outside of the Exosystem lies the 'Macrosystem', which comprises the child's culture, societal values, legal structures, and so on. These all affect the inner layers. A child who grows up in a very traditional society or community that strongly advocates the importance of children being reared by both parents and rejects the idea of parental separation and divorce, may well receive less support of a practical nature than a child growing up in a community that is much more accepting of separation and divorce. Within the Macrosystem, the ideological views that are historically dominant in the culture of an individual are viewed as being of great importance. Take, for example, children growing up in Northern Ireland where communities were, for many years, divided on the grounds of religion, or the southern states of the USA where generations experienced racial prejudice as part of their everyday lives, which in practice guided the thinking and education of whole communities of children and young people.

Bronfenbrenner identified a further layer, the 'Chronosystem'. The Chronosystem is about time and how it interfaces with those environments in which the child grows up. As children age, they interact differently with their environments and can become more engaged in managing aspects of their environment and those changes that they must negotiate as they grow older. Here, transitions are very important, for example starting nursery school, playgroup or primary school for the first time or, in other cases, the transition from a two-parent family through the separation and divorce of parents over an extended period of time. As transitions and chronological events occur, the child is developing not just physically and cognitively but emotionally, as well. It is worth considering how the Chronosystem has exerted influence upon Tracey and Ben as they make the transition to secondary school.

Bronfenbrenner's theory can be criticized on the grounds that it does not pay adequate attention to the individual psychological needs of children, as is the case with the work of Bandura. Take, for example, the experiences of children who have lost parents through divorce or, more particularly, those who have lost a parent through death and find themselves entering a stage of grieving. Whilst Bandura would focus upon the individual child's self-efficacy and learning modelled through those around him/her, which would underpin their resilience and coping mechanisms, Bronfenbrenner might focus upon the argument that grief occurs in all cultures and in all societies and, therefore, existing social and economic systems are in place to support the child.

Exercise

How might Bronfenbrenner's theory explain the impact upon young children of their parents' work patterns and lifestyles and how can his theory help practitioners understand the difficulties experienced by young children growing up with special educational needs and/or disabilities?

Summary

In attempting to further our understanding of social learning in young children, we can draw upon the work of a number of theorists such as Bandura and Bronfenbrenner. Their carefully considered and tested ideas and hypotheses offer effective frameworks to encapsulate and test our own ideas, thoughts and perceptions, from which we gain through our own personal experiences and learning. Bandura suggested that learning did not always involve change in behaviour and that children could observe others without their observations necessarily leading to changes in behaviour. He further suggested that motivation played a significant role in the link between observation and change in behaviour. Bandura saw motivation as a key factor in the development of children and young people and viewed self-efficacy as being central to educational development. Bronfenbrenner saw societies and communities across the globe as undergoing radical change. He argued that world economies have changed radically and we now have much greater emphasis upon the technological factors that drive our economies, but much of our working practice has not changed in tandem leading to enormous stress being experienced by many parents. Bronfenbrenner proposed that research into child development should take account of wider economic, social and political factors.

Table 6.1 Similarities and differences between Bandura and Bronfenbrenner

Similarities	Differences
Both Bandura and Bronfenbrenner acknowledge the part played by wider influences in society.	Bronfenbrenner placed much greater emphasis upon indirect influences such as the family environment and the community. He also viewed wider factors in society, such as the economic and political climate, as having a major influence upon children's learning and development.
Whilst not fully accepting the principles set out by more traditional behaviourists, they both emphasize the significance of social learning.	
They both viewed children's social interactions with others around them as being central to learning and development.	Bandura placed greater emphasis upon children's cognitive development, especially in terms of them acting upon information received from their environments. Unlike Bronfenbrenner, Bandura emphasized the importance of children imitating and identifying with others around them.
They both saw culture as playing a significant part in the education and schooling of children.	
Both theorists were also similar in that they did not view children's development in terms of stages.	Bandura placed greater emphasis upon self-efficacy than Bronfenbrenner.

RECOMMENDED READING

Bandura, A. (1997). *Self-efficacy: The Exercise of Control.* New York: Freeman.

This is a key text for any student or practitioner wishing to gain a much deeper understanding of self-efficacy and how it affects individual development.

Dowling, M. (2005). *Young Children's Personal, Social and Emotional Development.* London: Paul Chapman Publishing.

A useful resource for students and practitioners wishing to gain greater understanding of the social and emotional needs of children.

Miller, L. & Pound, L. (2011). *Theories and Approaches to Learning in the Early Years.* London: Sage.

An accessible and informative text, which will be of considerable help to students and practitioners wishing to develop their understanding of child development and the theoretical positions that underpin this most important stage in the lives of individuals.

REFERENCES

Bandura, A. (1977). *Social Learning Theory.* Englewood Cliffs, NJ: Prentice Hall.

Bandura, A. (1997). *Self-efficacy: The Exercise of Control.* New York: Freeman.

Bronfenbrenner, U. (1979). *The Ecology of Human Development.* Cambridge, MA: Harvard University Press.

Bronfenbrenner, U. & Ceci, S.J. (1994). Nature–nurture reconceptualized in the developmental perspective: a bioecological model, *Psychological Review, 101,* 568–86.

Buckingham, D. (2000). *After the Death of Childhood: Growing up in the Age of Electronic Media.* Cambridge: Polity Press.

Chapman, J. (2011). The collapse of family life: half of children see parents split by 16 as births outside marriage hit highest level for two centuries. *Daily Mail,* 18 April 2011.

Colverd, S. & Hodgkin, B. (2011). *Developing Emotional Intelligence in the Primary School.* London: Routledge.

Johnston, J. & Nahmad-Williams, L. (2009). *Early Childhood Studies.* London: Pearson Education.

Linden, J. (2005). *Understanding Child Development: Linking Theory to Practice.* London: Hodder Education.

Miller, L. & Pound, L. (2011). *Theories and Approaches to Learning in the Early Years.* London: Sage.

Smith, K.S., Cowie, H. & Blades, M. (2003). *Understanding Children's Development,* 4th edn. Oxford: Blackwell.

7 BRUNER AND DISCOVERY LEARNING/ CONSTRUCTIVISM

This chapter aims to:

- explore the contribution made to our understanding of education by Jerome Bruner
- explore the nature of the term 'learning' in relation to the work of Bruner
- examine how children represent the worlds they live in
- examine the relevance of Bruner's ideas for practitioners today.

Jerome Bruner (Born 1915)

Jerome Bruner was born in 1915 in New York, USA and is considered by many to be one of the leading thinkers of our time. References to Bruner's work can be found in most academic texts that address learning and development. Regarded by most academics working in the fields of education and psychology as a key theorist Bruner offered new ways of thinking about children's learning and how they are taught. For a time, Bruner worked with the US army during the Second World War and later worked as an academic at Harvard University.

INTRODUCTION

It is important when examining different theoretical perspectives to understand and acknowledge the social and historical contexts within which they were created, the contemporary context within which they are being applied and, perhaps most importantly, their purpose. To fail to do so would be to miss a vital element in the temporal evolution of thought.

Like all theorists, Bruner did not write and function within a vacuum. Theorists are an integral part of what they write about and their theories are influenced and formed by how they see the world, and by their own unique personal journeys through life. For these reasons, it must be said at the outset that Bruner developed his ideas and theoretical views at a time when the world and, more particularly, the country of his birthplace, the USA, was undergoing enormous social and political change. Racial tensions were evident across the western world with many children in schools in the USA being segregated because of colour and race. The USA was emerging from the aftermath of the Second World War and the Korean War and facing a drawn-out conflict in Vietnam. Materialism was on the rise and society was witnessing the emergence of the 'teenager'.

Bruner's purpose, it can be proposed, in developing his theoretical perspectives was, to some extent, about challenging the thinking of the time, which was in large part dominated by a legacy of behaviourism and psychodynamic perspectives originating in the works of Watson and Skinner, and Sigmund Freud and Carl Jung. Smidt has commented:

> What made Bruner unusual and special in terms of Western psychologists at the time was his recognition that meaning is not determined by the biological needs we inherit, nor is it determined by individual thought: rather, it comes about through an active search for meaning within the context of a culture. (2011, p. 10)

Bruner was also challenging many of the underlying ideas that policy and decision makers held in regard to the schooling and education of children at the time. Smidt (2011, p. 85) has further commented: 'Bruner said that we should treat education for what it is, and for him what it was was political'. The purpose to which Bruner applied himself was eloquently expressed some three decades ago by one of the author's professors:

> Bruner's thesis was that the study of children in problem-solving situations had concentrated too much upon the nature of the tasks and the stimuli presented to the child, and too little upon the dynamic qualities the child brought to the tasks in order to solve them. (Brown, 1977, p. 74)

To properly explore Bruner's thesis as well as the purpose of his work, we need to look more carefully at what we understand by the term 'learning'.

WHAT DO WE MEAN BY LEARNING?

'Learning' is a difficult word to define and yet it is used so frequently and by so many practitioners when they talk of their work with children both in and out of the classroom. Arguably, it is perhaps one of the most misunderstood words in popular usage within the field of education and is a term that is, all too frequently, surrounded by confusion. At the heart of this confusion lies a lack of specificity and clarity. What, for example, do we understand when a colleague tells us that a child has 'learned' their times tables or that a child has 'not learned' their spellings or is 'failing to learn' something. Should we not be more precise in our verbal exchanges with other colleagues and suggest, for example, that the child has, 'underlying processing difficulties' that are affecting memory and has 'acquired inappropriate and inefficient strategies to store information and then retrieve it'? With the child who has 'failed to learn' their spellings, should practitioners be more precise when verbalizing the child's difficulties to one another and focus, for example, on the child's actual functioning in the area of 'phonological processing'? To say that a child is failing to learn something is too broad a statement and requires far more careful consideration and analysis, and yet it is a term that is commonly heard. Such terms need to be more explicit and specific.

To properly understand 'learning' is to demonstrate knowledge and understanding of theoretical positions (as in the case of Bruner) that underpin the word's usage. This is not however, as straightforward as it might seem, as different theorists have different ideas as to what learning actually is. Smith, Cowie and Blades, for example, have defined learning as follows:

> Learning refers to the influence of specific environmental information on behaviour. Within a wide range of variation, the way an animal behaves depends on what it learns from the environment. Thus, individuals of a species may differ considerably in their learnt behaviour patterns. (2003, p. 34)

It is interesting to note that Smith et al. include the words 'environmental' and 'species'. More interestingly, they include the word 'behaviour' and the term 'behaviour patterns'. In addition, Smith et al. appear to place emphasis upon the notion of humans being a species, as in the case of animals. Such a view is very much in keeping with the behaviourist tradition and places particular emphasis upon changes in behaviour being central to the notion of learning. It is very different to how Bruner saw learning, as we shall see later.

The work of the early behaviourists, as discussed in Chapter 3, introduced us to a way of explaining learning in terms of stimuli and responses and the importance of identifying observable behaviours and subsequent reinforcement. In attempting to offer greater clarity to our understanding of the term learning, however, the psychologist David Fontana has made reference to 'descriptions' of learning in which he makes an important distinction between the behaviourist tradition (more directly, the notion of *operant conditioning*) and the cognitive tradition (more directly, the notion of *instrumental conceptualism*). Drawing directly on the work of Bruner, Fontana commented thus:

> This somewhat intimidating title (Instrumental Conceptualism) is used by Bruner to define one of the most coherent and consistent cognitive descriptions of learning and still one of the most useful for teachers … Learning … is not something that happens to individuals, as in the operant conditioning model, but something which they themselves make happen by the manner in which they handle incoming information and put it to use. (1995, p. 145)

Having a clear understanding of what learning is, therefore, and those cognitive processes that underpin it is important for all practitioners working with children (Hayes, 2008). Equally important, however, is the need for practitioners to have a clear understanding of how behaviours are learned and subsequently reinforced.

Exercise

Identify a number of different situations where you have observed children learning and consider how they were handling incoming information from other children and adults and putting it to use. First, however, consider what is meant by 'incoming information'.

HOW CHILDREN REPRESENT THEIR WORLD

Bruner did not view learning as something that happens to individuals but more as a process in which the individual is actively engaged. This idea is central to Bruner's theory of learning and differs markedly from that of the early behaviourists who saw learning more in terms of stimuli and responses. For those working with children, the key difference is that Bruner is chiefly concerned with what occurs within an individual's thinking between stimuli being emitted and the individual making a response. He is, in other words, concerned primarily with those cognitive processes that underpin and direct the actions of individuals.

Bruner was interested in the 'strategies' that children use when they are learning and, more specifically, when they are engaged in problem-solving tasks and experiences that underpin and lead to concept formation. Whilst the behaviourists were concerned essentially with how children's reactions to stimuli manifest themselves, Bruner was more concerned with how stimuli are represented through symbols and words and how these representations facilitate generalization and connection with other concepts. Representing stimuli in this way, i.e. through words and symbols, was, Bruner suggested, of a much higher order and he saw the inferences that children make through symbols and words as being key to their learning and cognitive development, and he referred to this as the *Symbolic* mode. At the heart of Bruner's theory is the idea that individuals represent the world they live in, and their learning, through three 'modes'. He referred to these as: the *Enactive* mode, the *Iconic* mode and the *Symbolic* mode, which has just been referred to.

The *Enactive* mode is concerned with actions, the *Iconic* mode with images and pictures, and the *Symbolic* mode, as we have just seen, which is far more complex, is concerned with words and symbols, and language. These modes do not follow on from one another as, for example, in the stages suggested by Piaget but, instead, are integrated with one another. In the *Enactive* mode, for example, an infant's sight of an object is unavoidably linked with their physical movements and behaviours. Take, for example, an infant in a cot who is given a rattle. The infant will shake it and be alerted to the noise it makes. Each time the infant is given the rattle, s/he will shake it. In this way the actual movements being made become encoded within memory through the infant's reflex movements and through what some practitioners now refer to as *kinesthetic* or *muscle memory*, and are linked to the infant's sight of the rattle. The child's concept of the rattle, therefore, becomes internally represented as a combination of noise, image and physical movement. The *Enactive* mode is, however, limited in that the infant cannot make links to other types of rattle. In this respect, the concept of 'rattle' for the infant remains located with the object upon which the infant is actually focusing. Such learning, it should be noted, is not restricted to infants and the internal representations that we make as infants can remain with us throughout our lives.

With the *Iconic* mode, a child can internally represent an object in the form of an image. Being able to do this allows the child to develop their cognition significantly. Having the ability to create and hold images means that the child can now apply their internal processing or thinking to objects that are not actually present in their environment. As with the *Enactive* mode, however, the *Iconic* mode has its limitations. Images formed by the child will be restricted to observable characteristics of an object, for example its colour, contours, textures and smell. Whilst the child may form internal images of their toys or their brothers and sisters, they will not be able to internally represent higher order concepts of, for example, kindness, joy, happiness and playfulness. They will need to internally represent these through language, which lies at the core of the *Symbolic* mode. Brown (1977) explains the difference between icons, or images, that are central to the *Iconic* mode and symbols, which are central to the *Symbolic* mode, as follows:

A photograph or a model of a cow would be an icon in that it would represent the animal in a very real and obvious way. The symbols C-O-W have no such characteristics. They only signify the existence of the animal by consensus of those who use the word. By eliminating the idiosyncrasies or special characteristics (for it will have to represent *a* cow) the symbol enables us to work with a general concept unrestrained by particulars. (Brown, 1977, p. 75)

Exercise

Identify examples of the *Symbolic*, *Iconic* and *Enactive* modes that you have encountered in your own experience with young children, and consider how they have facilitated new learning and thinking.

THE IMPORTANCE OF LANGUAGE

In drawing particular attention to Bruner's views of the function of language in young children, Smidt commented:

> Bruner reminds us that, 'Children learn to use language initially … to get what they want, to play games, to stay connected with those on whom they are dependent. In doing so, they find the constraints that prevail in the culture around them embodied in their parents' restrictions and conventions'. (Bruner, 1983, p. 103). (Smidt, 2011, p. 66)

As language develops, children increasingly remove themselves from situations by way of their thinking. They can, for example, engage with others in talking about situations elsewhere, about experiences they have had in the past, and might have in the future, and so on. Very importantly, they can engage with others in problem solving and critical reflection, both of which are fundamental to higher order thinking as proposed by Bruner. This developmental process is of enormous importance to early years practitioners and primary school teachers who create the linguistic environments for their children and who provide them with the opportunities to develop their language in tandem with their thinking. Take the case of Sally who is in her third year at primary school.

Sally is working in a group of five with her friends, Caroline, Michael, Julie and Mark. Her teacher has asked the class to work on a group task. Each group is given a single piece of A4 paper and a heavy textbook. The challenge for each group is to balance the book upon the paper. The children quickly become involved in the task and make random attempts at solving the problem. Though the teacher is interested in the strategies the children employ, she is more interested in the language they use. She listens to Sally's group as they work on the task:

Michael: 'This is mad, we can't do this.'
Mark: 'Yeah, no one can do this, it's stupid.'
Michael: 'Yeah, it's stupid.'
Sally: 'Wait, what if we change the shape of the paper?'
Julie: 'Yes, good idea. I know … what if we fold the paper like in a zigzag shape?'
Sally: 'Yeah, supposing we turn the paper on its side in a zigzag and then balance the book on top, that will make the paper stronger.'
Caroline: 'That's right. That will do it.'

At this point, the group achieves success and by folding the paper in a concertina shape and standing it on its side, they can easily balance the book. This example illustrates very well the importance of the *Symbolic* mode and how it facilitates more sophisticated thinking. By beginning her sentence with 'Wait, what if …', Sally is engaging in hypothetical reasoning, which is higher order thinking than that of Michael and Mark who are simply reacting to the problem they have been presented with. Sally, on the other hand, is putting forward a hypothesis, which will be tested not only by her attempts at manipulating the materials before her but also by the responses and reactions of the others, such as, for example, Julie's response to Sally's suggestion to change the shape of the paper. Here, Julie is confirming Sally's original hypothesis. In this example, Sally and Julie have engaged in higher order thinking, which goes much further in facilitating effective problem solving. The type of verbal support given by Julie to Sally is also reinforcing Sally's sense of confidence in herself and her own abilities to take risks in front of others and try out new ideas.

At the very heart of this example is language, and it is through the carefully exercised use of language in such situations that a child's potential becomes increasingly realized. For this reason, the contexts and experiences that practitioners create for children to learn, the development of vocabulary and the techniques they employ when questioning and explaining are vitally important. It is essential, therefore, that practitioners working with young children take time to reflect upon their own use of language, in particular the types of questions they pose and the vocabulary and phrases they employ, as well as the situations they create in order to analyse their children's language and thinking processes. It is through the contributions made by such theorists as Bruner that we gain insights into the thinking and learning of young children and come to use theoretical frameworks within which we can explore our own practice and that of others.

It is worth emphasizing at this point, however, that there are many children who struggle with aspects of language and who can, for example, hold only a very small number of instructions and directions in Working Memory before losing the thread of what is being asked of them. For these children, many of whom will have learning difficulties of a specific nature arising, from such conditions as dyslexia or dyspraxia, the early years practitioner will need to be especially vigilant. They will need to closely observe the actual responses of these children to their verbal instructions, questions and explanations, and, most importantly, the child's degree of understanding. Bruner saw the role of practitioners, therefore, as crucial to providing a system of support to facilitate and extend language development and he believed that language provided the central means by which children could develop their thinking and learning. Language, he argued, enabled children to internally represent their learning in sophisticated ways which facilitated abstract reasoning.

Directly related to the development of language is the emergence of literacy. In order for young children to read and write, they need to be able to recognize written symbols and the sounds that are attributed to these symbols. Indeed, Bruner (1975) took great care to emphasize the importance of both reading and writing in the cognitive development of young children. He even went as far as suggesting that the cognitive structures of children who engage more in these two processes will typically be different to those of children who engage much more in less language-orientated processes such as drawing and making things using solid materials (Brown, 1977). Bruner also suggested that this latter type of child typically differed from those who tended to engage themselves largely in talking with others. The rationale for his views was that, whilst all young children engage in basic language interaction with others, this does not, as in the case of children who engage a lot in speaking and listening, have any very significant effect upon the development of the internal representations of their thoughts. However, when young children engage in creating written symbols, which represent their own as well as others' speech and language, then an important transformative process occurs.

By representing thinking in written form, either using words or mathematical symbols, the young child can then engage in higher order processing or thinking whereby they can, in turn, engage in analysis of the ideas they have produced and represented through symbols. Clearly, this suggests that making marks, as very young children readily and naturally do, is an important element in their development and one that must be encouraged by the adults responsible for them.

A further and important dimension of children's language and thinking that Bruner came to increasingly recognize was narrative. Smidt has drawn attention to Bruner's emphasis upon narrative as follows:

> For the past two decades Bruner has been systematically developing what some call a narrative view of culture and mind and has argued that reality is itself narratively constructed. (2011, p. 92)

The crucial role that narrative plays has been recognized for some time and is central to the thinking of many leading thinkers and theorists. It was, for example, recognized by Steiner (Chapter 2) over a century ago and continues to inform practice in Steiner Waldorf schools today. With regard to the importance of narrative, Smidt has further commented:

> The reason children become narrators is because they explore the expectations they have developed about how the world should be. They develop these expectations through their experiences and their interactions and the ways in which they look for patterns and regularities in the world. (2011, p. 99)

As we have seen, Bruner interpreted narrative in terms of 'reasoning', proposing that '... reality is narratively constructed' (Smidt, 2011: 13). This concept of narrative is immensely important for early years practitioners who are involved daily in the life events and unfolding stories of their children. Each day, early years practitioners and teachers are drawn into and involve themselves, wittingly or otherwise, in the narratives children create of their own lives. They do this at a number of levels, and in doing so they can exert enormous influence over their children. To many practitioners, this process is not, however, always readily apparent and, more typically, not fully understood.

Practitioners and their children share with one another on a daily basis, verbal accounts of events experienced by themselves not only in relation to each other but also in relation to those significant others who are central to their lives. In doing so, the adults, it can be argued, play a central role through the medium of language in the construction of their children's knowledge, but perhaps more importantly they become involved in that subtle process whereby their children define and redefine the worlds within which they live. It is by understanding this process and fully acknowledging their part within it that practitioners can, with confidence, further define themselves as effective teachers and their children as effective learners.

Given that this process occurs as an integral functioning of day-to-day interactions, then it can be suggested that the process also offers excellent opportunities for practitioners to explore many hidden but important aspects of their children's social and emotional functioning, as well as their learning. More excitingly, narrative offers the practitioner a medium whereby insights and explanations of their children's life stories can be meaningfully related, understood and evaluated by themselves and others. By doing so, the practitioner can gain further insights into their own practice and their chosen pedagogies as well as their understanding of the nature of learning and problem solving.

BRUNER AND EDUCATION

In regard to education, Bruner took great care to emphasize the importance of culture, which he argued shaped our thinking and the manner in which we construct our understanding of ourselves and the world in which we live. In this respect, his views relate closely to those of Bronfenbrenner discussed in the previous chapter. In fact, Bruner saw schools as being only part of this process by which culture inducts the child, and saw cultures as being:

> made up of institutions (such as schools, hospitals, universities, libraries, banks, companies, shops, law courts, legal systems and more) where the roles that people can play are determined and where the respect accorded to these roles is worked out. (Smidt, 2011, p. 85).

Bruner suggested that we can only really make sense of what happens in schools when we view them within the wider context of the aims and intentions that societies have for their young, and he saw our conceptions of education as being a direct function of our conceptions of culture and its aims (Bruner, 1996). Take, for example, practitioners working in an inner-city area of extreme socio-economic disadvantage, who may well find that the popularly acknowledged aims of the surrounding culture are very different to those they might find, for example, when working in the pre-prep department of an expensive fee-paying public school.

Bruner viewed the manner in which children are supported with their learning in schools as being central to the development of their thinking and learning, and the development of their potential. Unlike Piaget, for example, who saw children moving through a number of stages during which their levels of cognitive development facilitated new learning, Bruner suggested that children could, in practice, be very involved in moving their own learning forward by undertaking more demanding and challenging tasks, provided they were properly supported.

Example

Angela has started her second year at primary school. Her teacher has decided to work on subtraction and has asked her class to complete a series of written numerical operations, which involve taking smaller single numbers from larger single numbers, such as 3 from 6. Angela completes these without any mistakes as she is using blocks to help her. Next day, the teacher asks Angela to complete numerical operations that require her to take smaller single numbers from larger double numbers such as 3 from 10 and 6 from 14. Angela becomes confused because the digits on the top row are smaller than the single digit on the lower row. The teacher comes to help Angela and introduces her to a method whereby she borrows and carries using the different columns. Angela performs this method alongside her teacher and when she has successfully completed two examples her teacher leaves her to help another child. The lesson finishes and the teacher does not introduce her class to further number work until a week later. By this stage, Angela has forgotten the method taught to her and when asked to complete some similar numerical operations, becomes confused.

Whilst Angela was able to carry out the method in the previous week, she has not conceptualized it. The problem is, in fact, too abstract for her and she has not been able to make the necessary steps to link it to existing internalized cognitive structures. The gap between these has been too great and she ought to have been directed to use much smaller graded steps, and have lots of reinforcement and over learning, which would have led to more effective learning and better retention, and subsequent recall. In effect, she needed more sustained support from her teacher over time with internalizing and accommodating her new learning as she progressed through a range of small steps.

It might be suggested that Bruner applied something of Vygotsky's thinking to educational settings. One example of this is Bruner's notion of 'scaffolding'. Whilst Vygotsky had offered insights into how adults supported children in their learning and, particularly, in their ability to reflect, he had not been specific as to how this might be managed by, for example, practitioners working with children. To this extent, his views remained very much of a theoretical nature. In practice, scaffolding is happening everywhere around us. We see parents structuring activities for their children, older siblings or friends structuring tasks for younger members of the family and attentive grandparents patiently taking their young grandchild through sequences of activities, which they have broken down into small steps and which they explain carefully along the way. It can typically be seen where older brothers or sisters are modelling and teaching their younger siblings to develop new skills and knowledge such as knowing how to whistle, climb over rocks, and so on.

Though scaffolding offers structure to learning, it does not imply a rigid structure. Take, for example, the very young child in a playgroup situation who plays or works alongside an adult. The adult models a particular activity and is observed by the young child who will then respond to the adult's spoken encouragement to try new strategies for solving a particular problem. In this case, the adult might also break down the child's learning into smaller, more manageable elements. In a sense, the adult is offering the child a scaffold, which will allow him to extend his knowledge and skills, and, perhaps more importantly, his understanding. As the adult breaks down the task and guides the child in attempting new ways of problem solving using different strategies, then the child will typically become more absorbed in the task; this sustains motivation, which in itself can then be even more motivating for the child.

Closely linked to learning in more formal educational environments is the notion of motivation and the degree to which learners are interested in the tasks they are being asked to complete. Bruner viewed children's levels of interest in a subject as being one of the best stimuli to their learning. He saw the role of the teacher, therefore, as being very much about encouraging children to become actively, and purposefully, involved in what they do. By doing so, children become more intrinsically motivated. In other words, they become engaged because they want to be and because they experience inner feelings of satisfaction. This process is vitally important for children's future learning in the early years because it lays down foundations for the way in which children will approach learning tasks in more formal settings when they attend primary and then post-primary school. This process is also closely linked to the development of self-efficacy discussed previously in relation to Bandura, and the role of the teacher as 'mediator' proposed by Feuerstein and discussed later in Chapter 9. Unlike Piaget, Bruner saw the social and cultural aspects of schools and early years settings within which children develop and learn as being of much greater significance.

A further important feature of Bruner's work is the importance he placed upon learning through discovery and by engaging in problem solving. Here, the child uses their previous knowledge and life experiences to build new knowledge and skills and further develop their thinking. Discovery learning is viewed by those who strongly advocate it as being a means for strengthening the internalization of meaning and the conceptualization of new facts into existing knowledge. Smidt commented as follows:

> For Bruner, meaning has always been at the heart of any investigation into mind and cognition. When we talk of meaning we are talking about making sense of something, of understanding or comprehending it. (2011, p. 10)

On first consideration, some might consider the notion of learning through discovery as being a wholly good and beneficial thing. However, there are those who would suggest that there are a number of drawbacks. For example, children may, during their episodes of discovery learning, acquire misconceptions and these may go unnoticed by the adults managing their learning. In addition, discovery learning may suit some learning styles much more than others and there may be children who prefer to work in more didactic ways. Furthermore, there may be some parents and schools who view discovery learning as underused time, preferring instead that their children engage with more formal situations where information is directly taught and their children are expected to complete identifiable tasks and make identifiable progress in comparison to their peers.

CONNECTING WITH BRUNER IN THE TWENTY-FIRST CENTURY

What then can Bruner offer to practitioners in the twenty-first century and how can practitioners assimilate his ideas into their own understanding of what they do: Perhaps more importantly, how does having knowledge of Bruner's ideas impact upon practice? To explore these questions, we need to see the work of Bruner, as in the case of all of the theorists and philosophers we have encountered, within the context of the twenty-first century and our own immediate cultures, communities and internalized world views of the realities that surround us. Smidt commented:

> Bruner said that the world (and everything in it) is not just as you see it but it is as you see it in context and in relation to your thoughts. So things may look different depending on how you feel, who you are with, what you have just been doing, what you are thinking about and so on … There is a link between perception, mind and learning. (2011, p. 9)

What, then, are our perceptions of childhood and how realistic are these? It is now generally accepted that parents in modern industrialized societies typically spend less time with their children than did their own parents and grandparents, as was the case when Bruner was originally constructing his views on learning and development. This is, in part, due to the changes in working patterns over the last decades. James commented:

> Since 1998 the number of people in Britain working more than sixty hours a week has more than doubled (from 10 to 26 percent), and full-time Brits work an average of forty-four hours, the most in the European Union. (2007, p. 273)

Many parents now feel that because they are spending less time with their children, they should place much greater emphasis upon what they actually do with them (Buckingham, 2000). This perceived need has been driven, in part, it is argued, by an exaggerated sense of needing to 'up the quality' of the time they spend with their children. Indeed, Buckingham has also pointed towards the notion of this time with children as a commodity in which some parents feel that they need to be viewed by others around them as being heavily involved with their children. More recently, in the UK, the concept of the 'Yummy Mummy' has emerged and now offers a popularized term to represent a type of parenting characterized, some would say, by competitive parenting. Added to this is the number of children growing up in reconstituted families, which can bring its own challenges. Only a decade ago, 10 per cent of families in the UK with dependent children were stepfamilies (Johnston and Nahmad-Williams, 2009, p. 218). Such changes in the dynamics of family relationships and parenting are relatively new to us and, though similarities with previous decades can be observed, it is, nonetheless, important to recognize that the nature of these changes is now characteristically different. As such, we must take these into account when drawing upon Bruner's ideas to help us interpret and understand our own observations, perceptions and evaluations of how children are thinking and learning.

Play as a feature of young children's activities has also altered dramatically in the last decades. It is generally recognized that young children now play less outside of their homes so that their parents can keep a close eye on them. Many children spend more time nowadays watching television or engaging with electronic games, computers and the internet. According to Zwozdiak-Myers:

> there seems little doubt that the default for contemporary children's play is interior whereas for previous generations, particularly in the second half of the twentieth century, it was exterior. (2007, p. 6)

Given the emphasis that is now placed upon materialism and the use of technological playthings, and the need for parents to feel that they must spend more time with their children, it can be suggested that many parents have become prisoners of their children's demands. Bruner also emphasized the importance of children learning through the process of enquiry and encouraged practitioners to accept and feel comfortable with intuitive thinking as being an important element in learning. Such views, however, stand in stark contrast to actual practice in some areas of the education system. The popular author Oliver James, for example, has drawn attention to the pressure that many children are placed under by their parents and by the competitive nature of certain elements of our society:

> A London private nursery school was recently exposed in a newspaper as doing tests on two-year-olds to see whether they would be suitable for entry at three. The test was to leave the toddler alone in a room with five others; the ones that failed were deemed to be those who went after their mother when she left the room. (2007, p. 280)

Definition

Metacognition refers to a learner's knowledge about their own mental abilities such as memory and attention. For example, knowing you have a bad memory, you may write notes to yourself.

Directly related to this is the view (Fisher and Rush, 2008) that too many teachers of young children continue to overly concern themselves with the delivery of content and do not engage enough with those reflective processes, and metacognitive structures, which are at the heart of learning. In addition, it can be suggested that too many teachers and early years practitioners fail to give priority to these processes and structures of which they themselves are a dialectical part (Fisher et al., 2010). This being the case, many young children may well continue failing to have their individual learning needs met, and fail to reach their true potential (Long et al., 2007). Fisher et al. (2010, p. 94) have, for example, commented as follows:

> Students preparing to enter the teaching profession should have as a major priority the need to devote real time to embracing theoretical views on learning ... To do so would potentially free them from vague and distorted notions of what learning actually is and lead to much greater understanding of the nature and function of knowledge, the purpose of learning, and the manner in which individuals at different stages of their development process information and construct meaning of the world around them, and act rationally to improve their lives through effective learning.

Despite policy and decision makers continuing to debate theories of teaching and learning and how effective different pedagogies are, the central debate in the UK remains dominated by simplistic and polarized views of teaching and learning as being either traditional and teacher-led or modern and child-centred (Geens et al., 2009). It can be asked then, to what extent do the ideas of such theorists as Bruner really influence policy and decision making?

Exercise

Consider in which ways early years practitioners might need to develop their practice to meet the changing and diverse needs of young children in the twenty-first century.

Summary

It is important to fully recognize that theorists do not construct their ideas, propositions and theories in isolation to the worlds they inhabit. It is equally important to understand that practitioners need to view theoretical perspectives within their own immediate situations

(Cont'd)

(Cont'd)

and the cultures and societies in which they practise. Bruner, as we have seen, grew up in a rapidly changing society in the USA and, unlike Vygotsky, for example, had access to what some might argue was a freer and more open society. Whilst Bruner formulated his thinking within a society characterized by a growing sense of materialism, Vygotsky's thinking emerged within a society built largely upon a Marxist philosophy. Despite living in vastly different cultures, it is fair to say that Vygotsky had a huge influence upon Bruner's thinking and the way in which he shaped his theory. Perhaps one of the greatest differences between these two key figures though was Bruner's absolute belief in the importance of culture as being central to the learning of children. Like Vygotsky, Bruner has offered practitioners a great deal in terms of understanding those cognitive processes that underpin learning in young children. The subtle, but significant, differences between their theoretical perspectives again highlights the view that the term 'learning' requires careful consideration and reflection when used to describe and explain children's behaviours to others.

RECOMMENDED READING

Bruner, J.S. (1960). *The Process of Education*. Cambridge, MA: Harvard University Press.
Bruner, J.S. (1983). *Child's Talk: Learning to Use Language*. New York: Norton.

Both of these texts offer in-depth accounts of Bruner's theoretical perspectives. Whilst the former focuses upon the wider education process as envisaged by Bruner, the latter concentrates more upon the importance of language in relation to thinking and culture.

REFERENCES

Brown, G. (1977). *Child Development*. Shepton Mallet: Open Books.
Bruner, J.S. (1975). Language as an instrument in thought. In A. Davies (ed.) *Problems of Language and Learning*. London: Heinemann.
Bruner, J.S. (1996). *The Culture of Education*. Cambridge, MA: Harvard University Press.
Buckingham, D. (2000). *After the Death of Childhood: Growing up in the Age of Electronic Media*. Cambridge: Polity Press.
Fisher, A. & Rush, L. (2008). Conceptions of learning and pedagogy: developing trainee teachers' epistemological understandings. *The Curriculum Journal, 19, 3*, 227–38.
Fisher, A., Russell, K., MacBlain, S.F., Purdy, N., Curry, A. & MacBlain, A. (2010). Re-examining the culture of learning in ITE: engaging with the new demands of the 21st century. *Critical and Reflective Practice in Education, 2*, 92–102.
Fontana, D. (1995). *Psychology for Teachers*. Basingstoke: Palgrave McMillan.

Geens, W., James, S. & MacBlain, S.F. (2009). Journeyman to master: the changing shape of a PGCE Primary course. *The International Journal of Learning, 16, 8,* 629–40.

Hayes, D. (2008). *Foundations of Primary Teaching.* London: Routledge.

James, O. (2007). *Affluenza.* London: Vermilion.

Johnston, J. & Nahmad-Williams, L. (2009). *Early Childhood Studies.* London: Pearson Education.

Long, L., MacBlain, S.F. & MacBlain, M.S. (2007). Supporting the pupil with dyslexia at secondary level: mechanistic or emotional models of literacy. *Journal of Adolescent and Adult Literacy, 51, 2,* 124–34.

Smidt, S. (2011). *Introducing Bruner: A Guide for Practitioners and Students in Early Years Education.* London: Routledge.

Smith, K.S., Cowie, H. & Blades, M. (2003). *Understanding Children's Development,* 4th edn. Oxford: Blackwell.

Zwozdiak-Myers, P. (ed.) (2007). *Childhood and Youth Studies.* Exeter: Learning Matters.

DEVELOPING A NEW PERSPECTIVE: THE NEW SOCIAL STUDIES OF CHILDHOOD

This chapter aims to:

- outline the development of a new theoretical perspective variously termed the new social studies of childhood and the new sociology of childhood
- explore how this approach facilitates our understanding of the child
- highlight the strengths and weaknesses of this approach.

INTRODUCTION

Thus far, we have examined the philosophies and theories which shape our understanding of children's learning. A thorough perusal of the theoretical perspectives posited by Pavlov, Watson, Thorndike, Skinner, Piaget, Vygotsky, Bandura, Bronfenbrenner and Bruner reveals that no single theorist has offered a complete explanation of children's learning. Each perspective has strengths and weaknesses, and in attempting to understand aspects of children's learning, scholars typically draw on several learning theories. In recent years, discontent with the methods employed by developmental psychologists and the lack of attention afforded children and childhood by sociologists provided the impetus for the emergence of a new disciplinary approach variously termed the new social studies of childhood and the new sociology of childhood. These terms reflect the contradictory views of scholars currently working within this disciplinary approach. For Muñoz (2006), the new sociology of childhood is a sub-discipline of sociology, whereas for James (2007) the new social studies of childhood (NSSC) is a multidisciplinary approach which embraces contributions from a range of disciplines including psychology, geography, history, anthropology and sociology. Concurring with the analysis proffered by James, throughout this chapter we employ the latter term (NSSC) to denote the multidisciplinary nature of this newly evolving field and the contribution which psychologists such as ourselves bring to this field of study.

In placing the child at the heart of the discussion, we quite deliberately marginalize inter-disciplinary debates which, in positioning one discipline against another, cloud the central issue – young children's lives. The chapter begins with a brief overview of the history of childhood and the influences which have shaped and challenged societal notions of childhood. It continues by examining the methodological tools devised by scholars working within the NSSC. The final section explores the fit and tensions between the NSSC and conventional theories of child development. Table 8.1 at the end of this chapter provides a useful, though not definitive, summary of the strengths and weaknesses of the NSSC.

The study of children and childhood has a short history. In their seminal publications, both Ariès (1962/1986) and Zelizer (1985/1994) describe childhood as a modern concept. They point out that prior to the seventeenth century childhood was not perceived as a distinct category of life. On the contrary, children tended to be perceived as undeveloped adults or adults-in-waiting. By the time of the industrial revolution, a number of laws had been enacted to ensure the protection and later the education of children. In *Pricing the Priceless Child: The Changing Social Value of Children,* Zelizer notes that between the nineteenth and twentieth centuries, a transition occurred from perceptions of the child as being economically 'useful' to economically 'useless' but emotionally 'priceless' (Zelizer, 1985/1994). He suggests that the real 'value' of children lies in their ability to give meaning and fulfillment to their parents' lives. Whilst definitions of children are frequently based on biological distinctions, McDowall Clark (2010) disputes any suggestion of a 'universally agreed definition of childhood' (p. 8), pointing out that practices with regards to children vary from country to country and culture to culture. This is a view shared by Prout who observes how:

> The diversity of forms that childhood can take is expanding, or at least becoming more visible. As a consequence there is a need to revise the assumption that childhood is a unitary phenomenon. (2005, p. 3)

Social inequity appears in many guises, not least in global employment patterns. For instance, 14-year-old children can be employed on a part-time basis and 16-year-olds on a full-time basis in the UK. Compare this practice with evidence from a global report by the International Labour Force (2005) which reports that 246 million children worldwide are involved in child labour, and that 179 million children aged 5 to 17 are exposed to forms of child labour that cause irreversible physical or psychological damage, or that even threaten their lives. A further 8.4 million children are trapped in the worst forms of child labour, including forced and bonded labour, pornography, prostitution and armed conflict, and every year 22,000 children die from work-related accidents (Magliano, 2005). Consequently, many children in developing countries find their childhood and education curtailed at an early age by social, cultural and economic conditions. Yet the dominant construction of childhood in the developed world is of childhood as a time of innocence, play, education and economic dependence (Woodhead, 2005). Summing up his views on the diversity of children's experiences, Woodhead notes:

> While universal accounts of normal development offer a powerful basis for realising rights in early childhood, they also have limitations. Firstly, they tend to overlook the diversities in children's experiences, including differences in the ways children learn, play and communicate ... Secondly, any particular account of young children's development is always partial, and can never encompass the varieties of childhood. Thirdly, specific cultural patterns of early development and care risk being normalised and universalised. (2005, p. 88)

Recognizing that childhood is not a natural or universal feature has important implications for early years practitioners. Woodhead (2005) points out that early childhood settings are culturally constructed; they are dynamic and evolving social contexts with no two operating in exactly the same way. Children attending early years settings have rich and diverse life experiences which are constructed and mediated by their peers and the adults in their setting, who in turn are products of their own cultural history and circumstances which add structure to their lives and meaning and direction to their experiences.

Exercise

Consider the beliefs and cultural practices which shape your early years settings. How do they affect the children in the setting?

To highlight global disparities in children's lives, the United Nations declared 1979 the Year of the Child. By 1989, the United Nations had published the *Convention on the Rights of the Child* (UNCRC, 1989). By 2009, this rights-based treaty had been ratified by 194 member states, the exceptions being Somalia and the USA. In accepting the Convention, member states agreed to adopt the 54 articles and two optional protocols which afford children and young people substantive human rights including the right to protection from violence; to leisure, play and culture, to education and freedom of expression on all matters that affect them. Article 13 of the Convention asserts the child's right to freedom of

expression; this right shall include freedom to seek, receive and impart information and ideas of all kinds, regardless of frontiers, either orally, in writing or in
print, in the form of art, or through any other media of the child's choice. Despite
the almost universal ratification of the UNCRC, children's rights are not universal. Burr (2004) argues that the UNCRC reflects western values and a particular
model of childhood that holds no value in non-western countries. This is particularly evident in cultures which place an emphasis on the collective rather than
individual rights of its citizens.

Although early childhood was not specifically mentioned in the original UNCRC
document, this was later remedied and a set of recommendations was subsequently
included in General Comment No. 7 in 2005 and published in 2006. This asserted
that early years children have the same rights as others to express their views freely
and to have those views given due weight in accordance with their age and maturity (Lundy, 2007). Section 3 of the document highlights concerns that children are
not being given adequate attention by states in terms of their laws, policies and
practices. The UK government further endorsed these rights in the Children Act
(2004), Every Child Matters (2003) and the Children Bill (2004).

The growing attention afforded children and childhood led a number of sociologists to question the almost total absence and marginalization of children from
sociological literature (Muñoz, 2006; Ryan, 2008). Nikitina-den-Besten (2009)
attributes the failure of sociologists to examine the lives of children to the macro-
level approach typically adopted by sociologists who focus on global systems,
politics, economics and family life. Others argue that it is their lack of economic
power which has silenced and marginalized children, and women before them,
from sociological study (McDowall Clark, 2010; Smith, 2011). As the focus on children in research gathers pace, questions are raised concerning children's role as
active participants in the construction of society.

Definitions

Ethnography: a generic term for a set of research tools which places emphasis on uncover-
ing participants' understanding of their social and symbolic world.

Methodology: a system of principles or methods of procedure in any discipline, such as
education, research, diagnosis or treatment. They may include ethnography, experimental
approaches, action research or case studies.

Methods: the tools, materials or artefacts used to gather data.

THE EVOLUTION OF THE NEW SOCIAL STUDIES OF CHILDHOOD

As previously discussed, childhood is not a unitary concept. As sociologists began to question the lack of visibility of children in their research, they also queried the transmission and construction of knowledge. Christensen and Prout (2005) articulate the swift progression of thinking from children being viewed as a natural or biological phenomenon to being understood as products of 'history, society and culture'. Children were now seen as active participants in the interpretation and construction of their own cultural knowledge. As the focus shifted to examine children's lives, it became clear that it was more complex and intricate than had been assumed by some sociologists. By way of explanation, Giesecke (1985, cited in Christensen and Prout, 2005, p. 49) pointed out that children, like adults, live in a society of competing, complementary and divergent values and perspectives gleaned from the media, the consumer society and adult and peer relationships.

According to Muñoz (2006, p. 10), the NSSC has three key aims. First, it seeks to contribute to the social sciences in general by incorporating the voice of one of the most frequently forgotten groups in society: the child. Second, it aims to contribute to the multidisciplinary approach needed to address a complex phenomenon such as childhood by providing a sociological explanation. Third, to visibilize children as active social actors according to the principles of the UNCRC, it recognizes children as individuals with rights. Thus far, sociologists informed by this rights-based approach have focused on socialization processes or on the analysis of institutions responsible for this socialization: the family and schools. In adopting this perspective, sociologists focus on the processes which shape childhood rather than on childhood per se. The most influential approaches, to date, include:

1 The sociology of childhood: theorists working within this theoretical framework believe that the child should be the unit of investigation. Children are perceived as social actors and therefore researchers should focus on the relationships between a child's social world and the world of other children and adults.
2 The deconstructionist sociology of childhood: this approach explores societal beliefs about children and childhood. To understand the construct of childhood, these theorists attempt to understand how society transmits its notions to the child.
3 The structural sociology of childhood: this perspective considers childhood a distinct period in life. Researchers link significant aspects of the child's life (such as poverty) with macro-level contexts and attempt to explain them in terms of their significance to macro-level mechanisms (Muñoz, 2006).

Corsaro (1997) suggested another approach termed 'interpretive reproduction'. Advocates of this approach view the child as actively interpreting their cultural practices. Corsaro believed that children interact with a number of childhood cultures which are interconnected like a spider's web. He was one of the first sociologists to take early childhood as the starting point for his thesis on culture.

The methods employed by theorists working within these differing theoretical paradigms also differ. Whereas structuralists employ quantitative data gleaned from secondary sources, others employ qualitative ethnographic or individual and group interviews. Advocates of the NSSC eschew quantitative approaches to childhood research, typically preferring interviews with children and observations of children in their natural environment. Framing interview questions to avoid ambiguity or misinterpretation presents its own problems. Research suggests that, in the main, children do their best to please adults and will even answer questions that make no sense at all (Greene and Hill, 2005; McLeod, 2008). Hughes and Grieve (1980) asked children nonsense questions such as 'is red heavier than yellow?' and 'one day two flies were crawling up a wall. Which fly got to the top first?' Even though they made no sense, the majority of children attempted to answer these questions. Waterman, Blades and Spencer (2001) found that children are 76 per cent more likely to answer nonsense questions than adults (20 per cent). The reason why they attempt to answer such questions can be attributed to the phrasing of the question or to the fact that children are used to answering adults, who may not always make sense.

Recently, the first author conducted a series of focus groups with young children aged between 4 and 6 years of age. In preparation for these interview discussions, two groups of children agreed to act in the role of children's advisers to the project. The first task was to consider the form questions should take for our young interviewees. We asked whether we should use puppets, paintings, photographs or other methods to gain a real understanding of the children's experiences of the after-school club they were attending. Whilst older children aged between 9 and 10 years of age suggested role play, drawings, stickers and camcorders, younger children aged between 7 and 8 years of age suggested that we simply 'ask them. Just ask the questions and they'll tell you the answers'. One interpretation of this practical response is that adults and older children tend to over-complicate the interview process and to underestimate children's ability to understand properly phrased questions. As McLeod points out: 'the adult who wants to listen needs to learn to keep their mouth shut and their eyes and ears open' (2008, p. 106). Consider McLeod's point in terms of the following example drawn from the experiences of one early years practitioner in New Zealand:

I turned ready to free Lys from her clothing but was met by a serious attempt to remove her sweatshirt herself. Without any thought I began to aid Lys by shifting the bottom edge for her. Lys stopped; looked straight at me, making sure I was going to listen and stated boldly,

'No Lys'. Of course, I stopped immediately and was truly embarrassed by having doubted Lys's abilities. 'Sorry Lys', I apologized … She was working steadily on freeing her left arm. Her elbows had become entangled in the folds of the material, her face serious as she persisted in her struggles. My hands trembled … itching to help, but Lys had warned me, she could do it. I watched in awe as her gutsy persistence paid off. (Hatherly and Sands, 2002, p. 12)

The practitioner in this example assumed that Lys required help to remove her sweatshirt. Taking her cue from Lys, she stepped back and even though she was itching to intervene gave Lys ownership of the task. This example neatly demonstrates the reciprocal nature of learning from child to adult and adult to child. Greene and Hill (2005) also point to the shortcomings of observations of children which impose adult interpretations on children's behaviour. They argue that adults can never adopt a 'fly on the wall' approach or neutralize themselves. Their very presence may be sufficient to disrupt the specific behaviour they wish to observe. Rather than impose an adult agenda, it is possible, as the children in the example above suggested, to simply ask children to explain their behaviour.

In a recent study, we had children draw pictures of the places near their home where they like to play. The older children, between 7 and 8 years of age, drew pictures of the local park, the club, their street or playing fields. Younger children, between 4 and 6 years of age, tended to draw their house, their garden, their mum and their siblings. When asked why they had chosen to draw their house, one child explained:

See that's where I play. I can't go the park if my big sister doesn't go too. You have to cross the busy road and I'm not allowed to cross the road by myself. I'm not allowed, so I play at home with my mummy and my little sister. Sometimes my friends come in and I play with them or I play in the garden on the swing or in the street with my friends.

As adults, we might have concluded that the younger children hadn't understood the task. By asking the children to explain their pictures, we determined that they had understood but, for safety reasons, their play area was limited to their home, garden or the street outside their house.

Mindful of previous methodological shortcomings, Christensen and Prout (2005) believe the NSSC has made some progress in this area by moving the perspective away from child–adult relationships to explore children's interrelations and interactions with each other. They claim that contemporary approaches see socialization as a collective rather than an individual process. This is a notion contradicted by Frønes (1993) who argued that there is no single childhood but multiple childhoods formed by the personal experience and interpretation of culture and society. You will note similarities between Frøne's claim and the views penned by Vygotsky, Bronfenbrenner and Bruner, who agreed that children are not passive recipients of culture but active participants in practices involving them with others.

For Bronfenbrenner, context includes any group whose members share the same 'values and beliefs, resources, hazards, lifestyles, opportunity structures, life course options and patterns of social interchange' (1993, p. 25). In the main, sociologists are more interested in the macrosystem of Bronfenbrenner's Ecological Model discussed in Chapter 6, which includes the child's culture, legal systems and social institutions. In contrast, psychologists are more interested in the microsystem, which includes the child's interactions with their mother, father, friends, family and grandparents. Like sociology, in recent years a number of psychologists have examined the methods and tools used to study children's behaviour. To bridge these differing perspectives, researchers working within the NSSC devised new methodologies and tools of enquiry.

METHODS AND METHODOLOGIES

Although he was discussing psychological theory, Vygotsky (1987–1998) argued that new theories require new methodological approaches. Conversely, Christensen and James (2000) believe that research into children's lives does not require a specific set of tools. This latter view is contrary to the theoretical stance adopted by the majority of sociologists and psychologists who have grown increasingly disenchanted with the methods employed by traditional developmental psychologists. Opponents point out that laboratory and experimental methods objectify children. Additionally, they argue, these methods ignore the influence of culture and context on the child's behaviour and on their interactions with others. It is a quarter of a century since Hill (1997) drew parallels between psychological descriptions of infancy and factory workers. She asserted that the experimental approach favoured by psychologists tends to focus on the acquisition of skills in children which later develop into more complex skills rather than on the processes involved. She drew parallels between this approach and an assembly line, arguing that both focus on production and target setting. Similarly, Burman (2008, p. 22) criticizes psychologists who describe infancy in terms of 'the normal child, the ideal type'. She asserts that the information which informs these trends is from comparative scores of an age-graded population. Scores are summed and averaged to represent normal patterns of development. Consequently, the picture of normal development presented is little more than 'an abstraction, a fiction or myth'. Here you will note similarities between the views expressed by Hill, Burman and Piaget. Employed to test children's understanding of test items, Piaget became interested in how they came to their conclusions (process) rather than in their answers (product). He was the first to eschew experimental approaches in favour of observations of and interviews with children.

In the past, many of the research methods used by developmental psychologists were not child-centred and were heavily criticized on the grounds that scientific methods borrowed from the natural sciences were employed to study young children who were merely considered 'objects' rather than 'participants' in the research process (Burman, 2008). Similarly, it was argued that research was conducted 'on' rather than 'with' children. Within a social constructivist approach, however, the methods employed tend to be naturalistic, and methodological tools are employed for research conducted in real-world situations rather than in laboratory settings.

Over time, the distinction between method and methodology has become increasingly blurred. Since they represent two distinct aspects of research, at this juncture it seems appropriate to clarify them. A methodology may be considered a system of principles or methods of procedure in any discipline, such as childhood studies, education, psychology or sociology. It can include ethnographic or experimental approaches, action research or case studies. It is the methodological stance adopted by the researcher which influences their choice of method. Ethnographers, for example, employ a range of naturalistic tools including observations and interviews, whereas experimental researchers select materials that offer hard-core data such as achievement test scores, computer test scores, etc.

Researchers operating within the NSSC typically adopt the rights-based approach advocated by the UNCRC which introduces the challenge of finding an effective approach to elicit the child's voice. More recently, reflecting the multidisciplinary nature of the NSSC, a range of naturalistic and innovative tools have been utilized to engage children in the research process. Working with 3- and 4-year-old children in five European countries, Pascal and Bertram (2009) used multi-voice, intercultural, critical incidents, cultural circles (akin to circle time), story telling, wishing tree, listening posts, guided tours and focused observations, amongst other tools, to elicit the voices of children. Bitou and Waller (2011) worked with a group of 12 younger children, aged between 2 and 3 years in early years settings in Greece and England over a three-year period. Their methods involved participant observation, video and photographic evidence, walking tours and participatory games. To involve the children, the researchers frequently acted as novices who required the help and support of the children. Working with children with special needs and, in a few cases, limited speech, Gray and Winter (2011b) used thumbs up and down stickers, smiley faces and drawings to encourage children between 3 and 5 years of age to express their views.

Each of the studies mentioned above employed a multi-method triangulated approach to increase the rigour and fidelity of the research (Gray and Winter, 2011a). This approach is far from new and was originally introduced into research involving children by Piaget (1954). As well as the observations and interviews mentioned previously, he kept detailed diaries from his observations of his own children and devised tasks to test their understanding (see Chapter 4 for a discussion of Piaget's theory). As Moss, Clark and Kjørholt (2005, p. 5) point out: 'listening to young children requires of adults some revaluing and relearning of the hundred languages of childhood'. This notion receives support from other proponents of multiple, mixed method approaches to participatory research with children (Bussell, 2008; Crotty, 1998; Punch, 2002). Multiple mixed method approaches are argued to have a number of advantages over single method approaches (Clark et al., 2003). For example, the shortcomings of a single method approach are easily overcome when the same issue is explored using a range of methods. It is also believed that they produce more robust results, offer adults and children choice, and provide a framework for listening which can be focused on children's lived experiences embedded in real-world settings (Bussell, 2008; Clark et al., 2003).

CRITICISMS OF THE NEW SOCIAL STUDIES OF CHILDHOOD

The NSSC provided a welcome challenge to traditional research approaches involving children. Studies framed within the NSSC provide insight into, amongst many other areas, children's perceptions of their early years setting (Einarsdóttir, 2005a and b; Gray and Winter, 2011b), children's experiences of indoor and outdoor play spaces (Waller, 2006), children's rights to participate in the research process (Lundy, 2007; Te One, 2011) and the tools and methods used to release the voice of the child (Clark, 2005; Degotardi, 2009; Dunphy and Farrell, 2011; Holloway and Jefferson, 2000). It affords children rights previously denied them in research. No longer are they viewed as objects of study; instead they are increasingly involved as participants in the process. Anderson (2008) describes research undertaken to identify children and young people at risk of social exclusion, which involved children and young people between 5 and 13 years of age. They recruited and trained 15 young evaluators to undertake a series of interviews with children and to help with the analysis and interpretation of the results. Reflecting on the study, Anderson notes that peer interviews frequently lacked depth and that the quality was often poor. Nevertheless, the benefits of the process outweighed the challenges.

Gray and Winter (2011b) involved young children (3–4 years old) with and without special needs in every aspect of a small-scale research project from the selection of the topic through to the dissemination of the results. Reflecting on the process, they noted how they were continually required to negotiate access with the adults in the setting. Although permission was sought before interviews were undertaken with children and a full explanation given about the processes involved in the research, in two settings permission was refused to take the drawings the children produced during the course of the study or to keep any of the photographs taken by the children. Settings differed in the attention they afforded the findings produced by the children. Two encouraged the children to disseminate their results during the end-of-year graduation ceremony, one through role play and another as a presentation. Another setting had the children collate their materials in poster format and display it in a prominent position in the nursery. The last put the children's drawings on the wall but failed to act upon the children's findings. Similar to Burr's contention that countries differ in terms of their interpretation of children's rights, the same appears to be true of early years settings. Nonetheless, evidence suggests that research framed within the NSSC can go beyond eliciting data to supporting and scaffolding children's growing understanding. It also gives researchers an insight into the challenges which can preclude children from active involvement in the process.

Similar to the other research approaches discussed in this book, the NSSC is not without criticism. Whereas lip service is paid to children's views, McLeod (2008, p. 45) contends that the drive to include children in research led the UK government to introduce a torrent of initiatives which elevated listening to the voice of the child to a 'new orthodoxy'. Developing this point, Spyrou (2011) argues that the preoccupation with children's voices has led researchers to ignore the processes which produce children's voices in research, the power imbalances that shape them and the ideological contexts which inform their production and reception, or, in other words, issues of representation.

Despite claims that the NSSC is a paradigm, the approach is still in its infancy. At present, there is no ethical code or practice guide for researchers working within the NSSC. By necessity, researchers working within the field draw on the ethical guidelines of their own discipline which have evolved and developed over time to offer structure and guidance to researchers working with children and vulnerable groups. Sociologists can employ the guidelines established by the British Sociological Association; psychologists might prefer the ethical code set out by the British Psychological Society; whilst educationalists can draw from the code of practice developed by the British Educational Studies Association. Despite working with one of the most vulnerable groups in society, practitioners and researchers working within the NSSC are unregulated and lack a point of reference which would draw researchers together under the collective banner of the NSSC.

In terms of the focus of this text, in a thorough review of the literature we noted that researchers operating within the context of the NSSC do not address the development of learning or the hidden mental processes which support and extend the child's learning. We contend that practitioners working with children require some knowledge of the processes involved in children's learning so that they can support, develop and scaffold the child's development. We did, however, note that a number of scholars working within the broader context of early years have written about the development of young children's thinking and learning, including Abbott and Rodger (1994), Athey (2003), Donaldson (1983), Fabian and Mould (2009), and Nutbrown (1994/2006). In a text entitled *Extending Thought in Young Children*, Athey (2003) examines the quality of educational interaction between teacher and child, parent and child and parent and professional. Throughout the book, she reports evidence from research conducted at the Froebel Institute in London. Acknowledging the work of Piaget, Athey explores the development of schematic thought and how action turns into thought. Her work is heavily referenced by Nutbrown who also explores schema formation. She notes that:

> One of the clearest ways to understand progression in children's learning is to look at individual children over a period of time, observing their schematic interests, seeing how these relate to the development of their behaviour, their speech and their thinking. (2006, p. 37)

Definition

The microgenetic approach: This approach examines change as it occurs, thus attempting to identify and explain its underlying mechanisms. For example, observing a child solve similar problems over a period of time will enable a professional to identify the child's progress or repeated mistakes.

In this statement, Nutbrown concurs with Vygotsky's proposition that adults play an important role in progressing children's thoughts and appears to share his commitment to the microgenetic approach. This approach involves repeated observations of the same child over time. It enables a researcher to monitor small changes in children's ability on tasks over a prolonged period of time. Although time-consuming, it provides a rich insight into the child's development. By way of example, Pine et al. (2007) conducted a microgenetic study into the relationship between children's speech and gestures. Through close observation of 21 children, they surmised that children's gestures are rarely produced without speech and that there appears to be no correlation between the type of gesture made and the spoken word.

Exercise

Undertake a microgenetic study of a child in your setting for short periods of time over a week. Note the types of gestures the child makes and then observe the relationship between the child's gesture and speech. Are your findings similar or different to those reported by Pine et al. (2007)?

Summary

Few would dispute that children are active participants in the learning process. From birth, they interact, influence and shape their environment and the people who share that environment. In 1989, the UNCRC provided the tools for governments and policy makers worldwide to acknowledge the rights of the child to express their views on matters that affect their lives. This fuelled a new approach to research involving children as active rather than passive participants. Collectively, they provided the impetus for the evolution of a new movement which began in Europe and culminated in the development of a new theoretical framework termed the NSSC. Although it has had a profound effect upon the way children are viewed in the research process, this approach requires development and structure. In particular, it requires ethical guidelines for researchers working within this newly evolving paradigm. The strength of this approach lies in the multidisciplinary nature of this newly evolving field. In order to develop and grow, the strengths that each discipline brings to our understanding of children should be valued to ensure that we gain a rounded rather than narrow picture of child development. In essence, we believe that the strength of disciplines such as sociology and anthropology which explore the child's interactions with society and the collective can be complemented by psychology which takes the individual child as the focus of study.

Throughout this text, we have attempted to highlight the strengths and weaknesses of a number of key learning theories. We do not attempt to argue the superiority of any single approach but believe that each offers valuable insights into some aspect of children's learning. At this point, you may have a clear preference for a theory of learning or may feel conflicted and, like Nutbrown and Athey, prefer to draw on the strengths of several theories. In the final analysis, you may be forgiven for believing that further research is warranted if we hope to understand what goes on between the young child's ears.

Exercise

In Chapter 1, you were asked to consider which theorist best explains how children's learning develops. Has your opinion changed?

Table 8.1 Strengths and weaknesses of the new social studies of childhood

Strengths	Similar to:	Weaknesses
Adopts a child-centred approach. Children are viewed as active and powerful participants in the learning process.	Vygotsky Bronfenbrenner Bruner	
Emphasizes the role of culture and the environment in the child's learning.	Vygotsky Bronfenbrenner	
		Fails to explore covert processes such as learning, memory and attention.
Employs qualitative approaches including observations and listening to children as they complete tasks.	Piaget Vygotsky Bronfenbrenner Bruner	
Focuses on process rather than product.	Piaget Vygotsky Bronfenbrenner Bruner	
Recognizes the central importance of play.	Piaget Vygotsky Bronfenbrenner Bruner	
Identifies the importance of peer interaction and collaborative learning.	Piaget Vygotsky Bronfenbrenner Bruner	
Identifies the importance of developing the child's potential.	Piaget Vygotsky Bronfenbrenner Bruner	
		Considers the child at the collective rather than individual level.
		Lacks ethical guidelines for practitioners.
		Fails to regulate practitioners working within this new paradigm.
As a newly evolving discipline, it can draw on the best practice within a range of existing disciplines.		

RECOMMENDED READING

Kehily, M.J. (ed.) (2004). *An Introduction to Childhood Studies*. Maidenhead: Open University Press.

This useful resource explores how childhood is shaped by society. Contributors explore childhood from historical, socio-cultural and policy perspectives. Together with the present chapter it offers a useful insight into the factors that shape child-centred research.

REFERENCES

Abbott, L. & Rodger, R. (1994). *Quality Education in the Early Years*. Buckingham: Open University Press.

Anderson, M. (2008). Children's participation in program evaluation: a case study from the UK. Involving children in research (pp. 6–12). Compendium of papers and reflections from a Think Tank co-hosted by The Australian Research Alliance for Children and Youth and the New South Wales Commission for Children and Young People on 11 November 2008. Available at http://kids:NSW.gov.an/uploads/documents/InvolvingChildrenandYoungPeopleinresearch.pdf.

Ariès, P. (1962/1986). *Centuries of Childhood: A Social History of Family Life*. London: Penguin Books.

Athey, C. (2003). *Extending Thought in Young Children: A Parent–Teacher Partnership*. London: Paul Chapman Publishing.

Bitou, A. & Waller, T. (2011). Researching the rights of children under three years old to participate in the curriculum in early years education and care. In D. Harcourt, B. Perry & T. Waller (eds) *Researching Young Children's Perspective: Debating the Ethics and Dilemmas of Educational Research with Children* (pp. 52–67). London: Routledge.

Bronfenbrenner, U. (1993). The ecology of cognitive development: research models and fugitive findings. In R. Wonziak & K. Fischer (eds) *Development in Context: Acting and Thinking in Specific Environments* (pp. 3–44). Hillsdale, NJ: Erlbaum.

Burman, E. (2008). *Deconstructing Developmental Psychology*, 2nd edn. London: Routledge Taylor & Francis.

Burr, R. (2004). Children's rights: international policy and lived practice. In M.J. Kehily (ed.) *An Introduction to Childhood Studies* (pp. 145 59). Maidenhead: Open University Press.

Bussell, S. (2008). Research with children: thinking about method and methodology. Involving children and young people in research. Compendium of papers and reflections from a Think Tank co-hosted by the Australian Research Alliance for Children and Youth and the New South Wales Commission for Children and Young People, 11 November.

Christensen, P. & James, A. (2000). *Research with Children: Perspectives and Practices*. London: Falmer Press.

Christensen, P. & Prout, A. (2005). Anthropological and sociological perspectives on the study of children. In S. Greene & D. Hogan (eds) *Researching Children's Experience: Approaches and Methods*. (pp. 42–60). London: Sage.

Clark, A. (2005). Listening to and involving young children: a review of research and practice. *Early Child Development and Care, 175*, 6, 489–506.

Clark, A., McQuail, S. & Moss, P. (2003). *Exploring the Field of Listening to and Consulting with Young Children*. Research Report 445. London: Department for Education and Skills.

Corsaro, W. (1997). *The Sociology of Childhood*. Thousand Oaks, CA: Pine Forge Press.

Crotty, M. (1998). *The Foundations of Social Research: Meaning and Perspective in the Research Process*. Crows Nest: Allen & Unwin.

Degotardi, S. (2009). Relationship theory in the nursery: attachment and beyond. *Contemporary Issues in Early Childhood, 10*, 2, 144–55.

Donaldson, M. (1983). *Children's Minds*. Glasgow: Fontana/Collins.

Dunphy, L. & Farrell, T. (2011). Eliciting young children's perspectives on indoor play provision in their classroom: reflections and challenges. In D. Harcourt, B. Perry & T. Waller (eds) *Researching Young Children's Perspectives. Debating the Ethics and Dilemmas of Educational Research with Children* (pp. 128–42). London: Routledge.

Einarsdóttir, J. (2005a). Playschool in pictures: children's photographs as a research method. *Early Child Development and Care, 175*, 6, 523–41.

Einarsdóttir, J. (2005b). We can decide what to play! Children's perceptions of quality in an Icelandic playschool. *Early Education and Development, 16*, 4, 469–88.

Fabian, H. & Mould, C. (2009). *Development and Learning for Very Young Children*. London: Sage.

Frønes, I. (1993). Changing childhoods. *Childhood, 1*, 1–2.

Giesecke, H. (1985). *Das Ende der Erziehung*, 2nd edn. Stuttgart: Kiett-Cotta-Verlag.

Gray, C. & Winter, E. (2011a). The ethics of participatory research involving young children with special needs. In D. Harcourt, B. Perry & T. Waller (eds) *Researching Young Children's Perspectives: Debating the Ethics and Dilemmas of Educational Research with Children* (pp. 26–37). London: Routledge.

Gray, C. & Winter, E. (2011b). Ethics and participatory research with young children with and without a disability. *European Journal of Early Years Research, 20*, 3, 309–20.

Greene, S. & Hill, M. (2005). Researching children's experience: methods and methodological issues. In S. Greene & D. Hogan (eds) *Researching Children's Experiences: Approaches and Methods* (pp. 1–21). London: Sage.

Hatherly, A. & Sands, L. (2002). So what is different about learning stories? The first years. Nga Tut Tuatahi. *New Zealand Journal of Infant and Toddler Education, 4*, 1, 8–12.

Hill, M. (1997). Participatory research with children. *Child and Family Social Work, 2*, 71–183.

Holloway, W. & Jefferson, T. (2000). *Doing Qualitative Research Differently: Free Association, Narrative and the Interview Method*. London: Sage.

Hughes, M. & Grieve, R. (1980). On asking children bizarre questions. *First Language, 1*, 149–60.

International Labour Force (2005). *A Global Alliance Against Forced Labour Global Report under the Follow-up to the ILO Declaration on Fundamental Principles and Rights at Work 2005*. Geneva: International Labour Force Office.

James, A. (2007). Giving voice to children's voices: practices and problems, pitfalls and potentials. *American Anthropologist, 109*, 2, 261–72.

Lundy, L. (2007). Voice is not enough: conceptualising Article 12 of the United Nations Convention on the Rights of the Child. *British Education Research Journal, 32*, 6, 927–42.

McDowall Clark, R. (2010). *Childhood in Society*. Exeter: Learning Matters.

McLeod, A. (2008). *Listening to Children: A Practitioner's Guide*. London: Jessica Kingsley.

Magliano, T. (2005). The world's working children, *Catholic News Service*, posted 06.09.05 at www.freerepublic.com/focus/f-religion/1420002/posts (accessed 18 June 2011).

Moss, P., Clark, A. & Kjørholt, A. (2005). Introduction. In A. Clark, A. Kjørholt & P. Moss (eds) *Beyond Listening: Children's Perspectives on Early Childhood Services*. (pp. 1–17) Bristol: Policy Press.

Muñoz, L.G. (2006). The new sociology of childhood: contributions from a different approach. *Politica y Sociedad, 43, 1,* 9–26 (Translation from the original Spanish available at: www.enmcr.net).

Nikitina-den-Besten (2009). What's new in the new social studies of childhood? NHTEP, 5, 2009. Available at www.isras. ru/files/File/Inter/05/Nikitina-den-Besten_Eng.pdf.

Nutbrown, C. (2006). *Threads of Thinking: Young Children Learning and the Role of Early Education*. London: Sage.

Pascal, C. & Bertram, T. (2009). Listening to young citizens: the struggle to make real a participatory paradigm in research with young children. *European Early Childhood Education Research Journal, 1, 2,* 249–62. Available at: www.informaworld.com/smpp/title~content=t776628938 (accessed 10 January).

Piaget, J. (1954). *The Construction of Mality in the Child*. New York: Basic Books.

Pine, K.J., Lufkin, N., Kirk, E. & Messer, D. (2007). A microgenetic analysis of the relationship between speech and gesture in children: evidence for semantic and temporal asynchrony. *Language and Cognitive Processes, 22, 2,* 234–46.

Prout, A. (2005). *The Future of Childhood: Towards the Interdisciplinary Study of Children*. London: Falmer Press.

Punch, S. (2002). Research with children: the same or different from research with adults? *Childhood, 9, 2,* 321–41.

Robson, S. (2009). *Developing Thinking and Understanding in Young Children*. London and New York: Routledge.

Ryan, P.J. (2008). How new is the new social study of childhood? The myth of a paradigm shift. *Journal of Interdisciplinary History, XXXVIII, 4,* 533–76.

Smith, A. (2011). Respecting children's rights and agency: theoretical insights into ethical research procedures. In D. Harcourt, B. Perry & T. Waller (eds) *Researching Young Children's Perspective: Debating the Ethics and Dilemmas of Educational Research with Children* (pp. 11–25). London: Routledge.

Spyrou, S. (2011). The limits of children's voices: from authenticity to critical, reflexive representation. *Childhood, 18, 2,* 151–65.

Te One, S. (2011). Supporting children's participation rights: curriculum and research approaches. In D. Harcourt, B. Perry & T. Waller (eds) *Researching Young Children's Perspectives: Debating the Ethics and Dilemmas of Educational Research with Children* (pp. 85–99). London: Routledge.

Vygotsky, L.S. (1987–1998). *The Collected Works of L.S. Vygotsky. Volume 1: Problems of General Psychology. Volume II: The Fundamentals of Defectology. Volume III: Problems of the Theory and History of Psychology. Volume IV: The History of Development of Higher Mental Functions. Volume V: Child Psychology*. (Editor of the English translation: R.W. Rieber.) New York: Plenum Press.

Waller, T. (2006). Don't come too close to my octopus tree: recording and evaluating young children's perspectives on outdoor learning. *Children, Youth and Environments, 16, 2,* 75–104.

Waterman, A., Blades, M. & Spencer, C. (2001). Is a jumper angrier than a tree? *The Psychologist, 14,* 474–7.

Woodhead, M. (2005). Children and development. In J. Oates, C. Wood & A. Grayson (eds) *Psychological Development and Early Childhood.* (pp. 9–46) Oxford: Open University Press.

United Nations Convention on the Rights of the Child (UNCRC) (1989). *Convention on the Rights of the Child.* New York: UNICEF.

Zelizer, V. (1985/1994). *Pricing the Priceless Child: The Changing Social Value of Children.* Princeton, NJ: Princeton University Press.

9

THEORY IN PRACTICE: LEARNING AND THE REFLECTIVE PRACTITIONER

This chapter aims to:

- examine the importance of reflective practice in the work of early years professionals
- explore the social and economic context within which young learners develop
- look at key factors that are important in creating effective learning environments for young children
- bring together the concepts of learning and reflection as used in professional practice
- explore the relationship between theory and practice.

> ... systematically helping children to learn so that they are helped to make connections in their learning and are actively led forward, as well as helped to reflect on what they have learnt ... Practitioners teach children in many ways. The different ways to teach may be selected at the planning stage or may be a perceptive response to what children do and say ... The strategies used in learning and teaching should vary and should be adapted to suit the needs of the child. (QCA, 2000, p. 20)

INTRODUCTION

Underpinning the effective and purposeful teaching and learning of young children is the engagement by early years practitioners in critical reflection, and directly related to this is the importance of active and meaningful participation of children in what they do, as indicated by QCA in their above statement. With younger children, the activities they engage in, and the type and quality of their play, are crucial. Equally important, however, is the nature of the environments that are created for them and the extent to which they are encouraged to involve themselves in problem-based exploratory learning, both on an individual basis and, perhaps more importantly, with their peers and with the adults around them.

Whilst the concept of 'learning' was explored earlier, it is now also worth considering at this point what is meant by engaging in critical reflection, and why this might be so important for early years practitioners and teachers of young children.

Daudelin, cited in Zwozdiak-Myers (2007, pp. 160–1), has commented as follows:

Reflection is the process of stepping back from an experience to ponder, carefully and persistently, its meaning to the self through the development of inferences. (Daudelin, 1996, p. 39)

This definition is very useful as it points towards a number of concepts that can serve as signposts for understanding key elements that underpin sound professional practice with young children, namely: 'stepping back', 'carefully and persistently', 'meaning', and 'inferences'. These concepts are especially useful as they can provide an entry point through which early years practitioners can explore and evaluate their own professional practice. They also offer a means by which practitioners can engage in effective and purposeful evaluation of the learning they observe taking place around them, the opportunities they provide for their children and the environments they create.

What becomes quickly apparent when listening to effective early years practitioners and primary teachers is the nature of the conversations they have when talking about the children they work with. They are clear about the purpose of the environments they create and they know exactly what they are trying to achieve when they set tasks for their children. Conversations are typically characterized by meaningful and objective discussions and there is far less evidence of descriptive talk and narrated accounts when talking about learning, and about the individual needs of the children. The nature and purpose of these 'professional' conversations are extremely important and reflect a deep and systematic understanding of children's emotional, social and developmental needs as well as how they learn and in what contexts learning can be optimized. Effective practitioners take time to step back and carefully observe the behaviours of their children and take time to reflect upon their own behaviours and the purposes of their actions. They take great care when making inferences based on observations and they continually look for new meanings in what they do.

BECOMING A REFLECTIVE PRACTITIONER

It is always a point of debate as to whether we are born reflective or whether we acquire those dispositions that make us reflective. A useful entry point to this debate can be found in the work of Reuven Feuerstein (Feuerstein et al., 1979, 1980) who drew heavily upon the original ideas of Vygotsky. Before looking in detail at the work of Feuerstein, however, it is worth highlighting two crucial elements that underpin critical thinking and effective practice with young children, namely the nature and quality of practitioners' observations, and the importance of purposeful listening. One further element in critical thinking and effective practice proposed some decades ago by Schön (1987) is the need for practitioners working with young children to also have a deep knowledge and understanding of themselves.

The importance of undertaking purposeful and meaningful observation and listening is recognized throughout the literature. Dowling (2005, p. 30), for example, has commented as follows: 'The task of really getting inside children's minds and understanding them can only properly be achieved through observing their actions and conversing with them', whilst Penny Lancaster, writing in Pugh and Duffy, has suggested that:

> Listening to young children fits a rights-based approach in relating to children. It ... advocates a move away from viewing young children as passive recipients of adults' decisions, where choices and decisions need to be made on their behalf. (2006, p. 69)

Lancaster (again, cited in Push and Duffy) further suggests that in order to respect the child's voice, practitioners need to have 'understood how they [the children] have made sense of their experiences' (p. 72). This point is extremely important and emphasizes the need for early years practitioners to take time to 'really hear' what children are saying and to give their children 'space' in which they can process information at an appropriate level and within their own time. To fail to do so may well result in children learning to become passive agents in the adult–child relationships that exist around them. In extreme cases, such as with children who are experiencing significant social and emotional trauma in their lives, they may even fail to have their situations recognized and responded to. In the very sad and extremely severe case of the child Victoria Climbié, who was physically abused and then died, Penny Lancaster noted:

> Victoria Climbié needed someone to listen to her life experiences, her concerns, her feelings and her perspective of her situation, but no one did. Her rights were overlooked and the care she received was steered by adult demand. (p. 65)

Equally important to listening to young children is the need for reflective practitioners to develop their observation skills and to take time to understand and consider carefully what they are observing. Careful, considered and purposeful observation will inform and underpin effective planning, assessment and intervention, and will also facilitate the identification of appropriate learning objectives for the future. According to Cathy Nutbrown, writing in Pugh and Duffy, in respect of the importance of observation, argues:

> Observation and assessment are the essential tools of watching and learning with which practitioners can both establish the progress that has already taken place and explore the future. (2006, p. 99)

In reporting on observation in the classroom as undertaken by Montessori teachers, Feez (2010, p. 24) noted:

> When learning to observe, trainee Montessori teachers sit where they will not disturb, distract or interact with the children in any way. They record everything, including small details others might not recognize as being important. In particular, they record:
>
> - everything that interests each child, no matter how apparently insignificant
> - how long a child sustains interest in each activity they choose, whether for seconds, minutes or hours
> - how a child moves, especially movement of the hand
> - how many times a child repeats the same activity
> - how a child interacts with others.

This approach to the observation of young children can be used by practitioners as a model for their own practice.

Having recognized the importance of purposeful and meaningful observation and listening in the practice of early years practitioners, it is now worth turning to the work of Reuven Feuerstein who in recent decades has come to exercise significant influence upon many practitioners and academics working with and researching the learning of young children. Feuerstein's background was in clinical psychology and he studied at the University of Geneva under Jean Piaget and Barbel Inhelder. Following the Second World War, Feuerstein worked with child survivors of the Holocaust and went on to hold the position of Director of the Centre for Development of Human Potential in Jerusalem. Feuerstein has proposed that theories are based on those belief systems and values held by individuals within societies and that these belief systems are essential in the determining of action, which can be construed as effective. In this respect, it is worth early years practitioners taking time to reflect upon their own belief systems regarding childhood and how, for example, they might assess the intellectual functioning of young children and especially those children who present with difficulties in the areas of language and behaviour.

Feuerstein suggests that belief systems need to view human potential as having almost no limits whilst recognizing that artificial barriers remain in place which can work to prevent change in children realizing their potential. He further suggests that all children, no matter what their age and no matter what their degree of difficulty, can become effective learners. By adopting such belief systems, we can argue that early years practitioners and teachers become 'freed' from constrained thinking that limits their vision of what is possible for all young children. In doing so, they can be even more engaged in critical analysis of their own practice and the learning of their children. When this process is embarked upon, a number of consequences can occur, most notably recognition of the concept of what Feuerstein calls 'structural cognitive modifiability'. This refers to the belief that the brain's cognitive structure can be altered by an enabling process which permits the learner to 'learn how to learn'. Learning, essentially, becomes cumulative and affects performance throughout an individual's entire life (Burden, 1987).

Such an approach, Feuerstein argued, is directed at changing the structural nature of cognitive development. Feuerstein views 'structural change' in terms of an individual's manner of 'acting upon' sources of information and then responding to these. The central factor involved in learning how to learn is the idea of 'mediated learning experience' and it is this that underpins Feuerstein's *Social Interactionist Theory* of learning:

> the way in which stimuli emitted by the environment are transferred by a 'mediating' agent, usually a parent, sibling or other caregiver. This mediated agent, guided by his intentions, culture, and emotional investment, selects and organises the world of stimuli for the child ... Through this process of mediation, the cognitive structure of the child is affected. (Feuerstein et al., 1980, p. 16)

The crucial factors in mediating learning are: that the mediator must be aware of, make known and ensure the learner has comprehended what is intended (intentionality and reciprocity), that the mediator must explain why she is going to work at a task (investment of meaning), and that the act must be shown to have value over and above the here and now (transcendence) (Burden, 1987). It is important, therefore, for early years practitioners to reflect upon their own philosophies of teaching and learning and how they, themselves, mediate the learning experience of their children. How, for example, do early years practitioners, as mediating agents, select and organize the world of the child and how do they help the child to learn how to learn?

Exercise

Consider the difference between a child's 'ability' and their 'potential'. How might early years practitioners use the learning environment to develop each of these?

DEVELOPING YOUNG LEARNERS

Crucial to the practice of any early years practitioner is an informed understanding of development in the first years. Gaining an informed understanding of a child's development requires knowledge and critical understanding of the narratives that parents offer in regard to their children. Most parents are only too willing to talk at length and in detail about the events in their children's lives and in doing so they provide useful and relevant information about the early milestones in their children's development and even about possible causes for concern. Reflective practitioners can take opportunities when listening to parents to engage in careful and meaningful discussion, which will lead to better understanding not only of the child but also the home environment and the child's wider family and community (Johnson, 2010). In doing so, however, it is important for practitioners to critically reflect upon the inferences they find themselves making as a result of their discussions and observations. It is important to 'step back' and understand what parents are truly saying about their children. This has become increasingly important in the last decades as we witness huge changes in society.

The world into which children are now born is, perhaps more than ever, one of immense complexity, a complexity that we can all too often fail to properly absorb and comprehend (MacBlain and Purdy, 2011). How we understand and define childhood and, more importantly, the inferences we make about this time in the lives of individuals, are fundamental to sound professional practice. Miller and Pound (2011, p. 5), in making reference to the work of Kellet (2010), have emphasized that:

> childhood is a construction that arises from historical, cultural and economic conditions (Kellet, 2010) and … educators can hold multiple views or constructions of children … It is reflection which helps us to understand and reconcile what are sometimes apparently irreconcilable views.

Do we, for example, view childhood as a time of joy and excitement, fun and security, or do we, in the light of our own experience and that of others reported in the media, view it through less rose-tinted glasses and adopt what some might argue is a more realistic but cynical view?

As we set about reflecting upon how we might develop young learners, we also need to understand how children are influenced not just by their personal experiences, but also by the social, historical, economic and cultural contexts that surround them, which is at the core of Bronfenbrenner's theory discussed in Chapter 6. Across the globe, societies, communities and, perhaps more importantly, families, are changing at a rate unprecedented in history. It has been estimated, for example, that in the year 2001 in Britain there were some 3.1 million children living in lone-parent households (MacBlain and MacBlain, 2004). In the spring of 2002, it was further estimated (National Statistics, 2003) that one fifth of dependent children in Great Britain lived in lone-parent families, almost twice the proportion as in 1981. In the subsequent 10 years from 1981, the number of families headed by a single parent rose by over 70 per cent, with lone-parent families making up

19 per cent of all families in the UK (Brown, 1999, p. 66). This percentage is now much greater (MacBlain and MacBlain, 2004; MacBlain and Purdy, 2011). The rate of divorce has also been increasing at what many consider to be an alarming rate. Just over a decade ago, Rowntree (1998, cited in Brown, 1999, p. 66) predicted that 'If recent trends continue, more than a third of new marriages will end within twenty years and four out of ten will ultimately end in divorce'. Ten years before Rowntree's predictions, Wells (1988) estimated that in England and Wales alone, some 40–50 children each day lost a parent following bereavement. More recently, Holland (2001) has suggested that approximately 3 per cent of the school population will have experienced the death of a parent during their school years. Added to these two groups has been the increasing number of children in lone-parent households where parents have chosen to live separately and remain unmarried.

In effect, the structure of families is changing with many sociologists and educationalists now preferring to use the term 'households' instead of families. This has enormous implications for the early social experiences of children as well as their learning and emotional development. At the beginning of the twenty-first century, Buckingham (2000) alerted us to the fact that in Britain today there has emerged an 'underclass' where many children are failing to be properly represented. Buckingham has further alerted us to the fact that in the 13 years between 1979 and 1992, the number of dependent children growing up in households where income was not even half of the average income in Britain rose from one in every ten to one in every three. He also cites the incidence of children in Britain growing up in dwellings that are unfit for human habitation as being around the one million mark. This figure is now higher.

In reflecting upon the development of young learners, it is also important to acknowledge the influence of technology. Most young children, even some as young as 5 or 6 years of age, now have access to mobile telephones, computers, internet chat rooms and 24-hour television. One regularly hears of the concerns expressed publicly by organizations such as parent groups and teaching unions about the diet of violence and sexualized activity available to young children through different media platforms. In addition, there are significant numbers of children now entering early years settings and schools who have poorly developed listening skills and delayed language development, and who display a lack of maturity and preparedness for more formal learning environments (Palmer, 2006). The result of delays in language and immaturity also means, for many children, that they typically begin school at a disadvantage and can, in all too many instances, struggle with the acquisition of literacy and with forming purposeful friendships. In 2006, in a letter to the British newspaper, the *Daily Telegraph*, 110 teachers, psychologists and 'other experts' called upon the government 'to prevent the death of childhood'. The letter contained the following:

Since children's brains are still developing, they cannot adjust – as full-grown adults can – to the effects of ever more rapid technological and cultural change. They still need what developing human beings have always needed, including real food (as opposed to processed 'junk'), real play (as opposed to sedentary, screen-based entertainment), first-hand experience of the world they live in and regular interaction with the real-life significant adults in their lives. (Fenton, 2006, p. 1)

On the other hand, there are also significant numbers of children entering early years settings who have experienced high levels of input from their parents in terms of access to positive role modelling, educational experiences and sophisticated social situations, which aids them in developing their self-confidence and self-efficacy. Akin to this is the notion that young children have become a lucrative market. The young child in the twenty-first century typically now has much greater spending power than ever before. Only a decade ago, Buckingham (2000) estimated the size of the UK market for children's spending in the area of consumer goods to be in the region of £10 billion pounds. This is now significantly greater. Many parents and professionals now point to a run-away sense of materialism in the youth of today.

Exercise

Examine your own perceptions of childhood and consider how childhood might have changed over the last 50 years. To what extent do we see childhood as an idyllic time and should we be more realistic about our perceptions and examine more closely the life experiences of those children who are growing up in families where there is little emotional support?

CREATING A LEARNING ENVIRONMENT

The culture of early years and primary school settings has undergone massive change in the past three decades. There has, for example, been an increasing diversity of pupil needs as evidenced by the growing number of children now included in mainstream settings who have a wide and diverse range of special educational needs and/ or disabilities. In 2008, for example, it was estimated that in England alone there were approximately one and a half million pupils with special educational needs in schools, representing approximately a fifth of the school population. In addition, over 50 per cent of the 223,600 children (just under 3 per cent of the school population) with statements of special educational needs had been included within mainstream schools (DCSF, 2008). Moreover, in regard to linguistic diversity there are currently around 900,000 children in schools in England learning English as an additional language, suggesting that there are some 200 languages being spoken (MacBlain and Purdy, 2011).

Given the changing nature of the range of needs presented by young children in mainstream settings, it is extremely important for early years practitioners to reflect upon the learning environments, and particularly 'enabling environments', that can be created for all children and the degree of effectiveness or otherwise of these. In doing so, they can be guided by the work of theorists and philosophers against whose work they can compare their own thoughts, belief systems and practice. It would be useful at this point to look back at some of the key figures introduced in Chapter 2 and reflect upon how their ideas and philosophies of learning and development were so closely interwoven with the environments they felt were necessary for children to learn effectively. It is also worth reflecting upon how society has changed since they introduced their ideas and how society now influences our thinking about learning. Palmer has offered a sobering note in regard to young children entering schools in the UK and, perhaps, a challenge to early years practitioners about how they assist in the preparation of very young children for their future schooling:

> Everywhere I went it was the same story: four- and five-year-olds were coming to school with poorer language skills than ever before; they weren't arriving with the repertoire of nursery rhymes and songs little ones always used to know, and children of all ages found it increasingly difficult to sit down and listen to their teacher or to express complex ideas in speech or writing … I also discovered that this issue was bothering teachers across the developed world. (2006, p. 105)

As emphasized in Chapter 2, current practice in the field of education and learning has changed markedly within the last decade and will continue to change markedly over the next decades. Take the views of Dewey who advocated that school should be an 'extension of the home' or Steiner who saw the function of education as that of responding to the changing physical, cognitive and emotional needs of children. Set against significant changes in modern societies, with an increased emphasis upon technology and materialism, we can once again see the importance and wisdom of Steiner's ideas.

Equally, the pioneering work of the McMillan sisters, with their emphasis upon play outdoors and healthy living, can be viewed against recent legislation and practice in the UK regarding the importance of appropriate nurturing and care for children before they reach statutory school age. However, it should be noted that even in the latter part of the twentieth century much had not improved for young children in the UK. In addressing the situation for pre-school children in the UK during this time, Mayall felt able to comment as follows:

In the 1970s and 1980s, when other European countries were providing universalist high quality state-run nurseries, British pre-school children were (and still are) the victims of a ramshackle patchwork of poor services. Indeed ... they could not be called services, but rather an ad hoc system which operated certainly not in the interests of children, nor even of the people who ran them. (2002, p. 13)

Example

Arthur is 6 years of age and has just started his second year at the local primary school. He is struggling to acquire basic literacy skills in reading and writing, and appears to have particular difficulty with rhyming words and with words that contain several syllables. In addition, Arthur has marked difficulties with organization and with concentration and attention. He has been described by his previous two teachers as 'a real fidget' and as having 'very poor, almost no concentration span'. They have both emphasized to his new teacher that they constantly have to repeat instructions to him and that he is 'just too easily distracted by those around him'. His parents, on the other hand, emphasize how he can remain absorbed in construction activities 'for ages' and proudly tell their friends that he is 'brilliant at working things out in his head'. There are signs that Arthur is beginning to dislike going to school.

Arthur is typical of a number of young children in their early stages of formal education who are perceived as having difficulties when in fact they have failed to acquire suitable and efficient strategies for managing particular elements of their learning. Following assessment by an educational psychologist, Arthur was found to be predominantly a visual learner but with very poor short-term memory, which led to difficulties in following instructions given by his teachers when these were spoken quickly and in succession. At the time of assessment, he was also found to be intellectually very able with scores on a range of sub-tests falling in the superior range of functioning. Sadly, these key elements of Arthur's functioning were not identified with the result that poor short-term memory and underlying processing difficulties, which affected the speed at which he worked, were interpreted as poor concentration and organization, and as a general lack of motivation and interest. By the time Arthur was commencing his second year in primary school, he had already acquired and internalized a range of inefficient and ineffective strategies for accessing literacy and numeracy.

A major barrier to Arthur's progress is the perception that others have of him and the way in which his learning environment has been created, organized and maintained. Arthur has difficulty with the wide range of activities that are presented to him throughout the week and avoids planning ahead because this causes him anxiety and makes him confront his difficulties in this area. In addition, he is now perceived as not being very able and as a bit of a 'plodder'. Because he is forgetful and has difficulty attending to activities for long periods of time, he distracts others around him. This pattern of distracting has been learned and is being reinforced on a daily basis by the other children around him who observe him distracting others and laugh at him. The laughter is very rewarding for Arthur because it makes him the centre of attention and he enjoys the celebrity status that it offers.

THEORY INTO PRACTICE

As adults and practitioners, we typically explain social situations, the behaviours of children and their parents, and cycles of behaviour through our own internalized world views. We form opinions and we make judgements, which arise from our own experiences. All too often, however, these inferred judgements are more a reflection of our own emotional responses to others' behaviours, as opposed to careful and objective interpretations of what is, in actuality, happening. This of course has implications for the way in which we manage behaviours as well as social situations.

> ### Example
>
> Joe (aged 3 years and 6 months) is the youngest of three. He is attending a local pre-school. Joe's nursery school teacher has been concerned about Joe's behaviour and has referred him to the educational psychologist for assessment. When she met with the educational psychologist, she described Joe's behaviour as 'often unacceptable, he can be a real nuisance at times both to me and the other children. He is easily distracted and upsets the others, and on occasions his behaviour can be dangerous. Joe has almost no concentration and cannot stick at something for more than two minutes'.

What is interesting about the comments made by Joe's teacher is that they tell us little of any use about Joe. Instead, they are more a reflection of the teacher's emotional responses to Joe's behaviours. In this situation, the educational psychologist will be left with very little understanding of Joe's actual behaviours, what triggers them and how his behaviour patterns are reinforced. The educational psychologist will have to probe the teacher much further and take time to observe Joe in the classroom situation as well as outside of the classroom during unstructured time to gain objective information.

Drawing on theory to critically reflect upon one's own work with children is a vital element in ensuring best practice. It is theory and research that guides us with our understanding and knowledge and allows us to challenge not only our own ideas but those of others, in informed and meaningful ways. To illustrate this point, it will be useful to focus upon some specific aspects of one notable thinker who has influenced thinking and practice in the development of young learners. The work of Montessori lends itself to such a proposition. This is not to exclude others who have also exercised considerable influence as in the case of Froebel who has been referred to, for example, by Miller and Pound (2011, p. 64) as follows:

> Froebelians continue to influence official documents in a behind-the-scenes way ... from the Hadow report (1933) onwards, through to Plowden (Central Advisory Council for Education, 1967); *Starting with Quality* (DES, 1990); *Curriculum Guidance for the Foundation Stage* (DfEE, 2000); *Birth to Three Matters* (DfES, 2002); *The Early Years Foundation Stage* (CCSF, 2008).

Miller and Pound have drawn further attention to the more recent emergence of Froebelian training, which they contextualize as follows:

> Given the central control of teacher training, and the move towards this for other practitioners in the early childhood field, the Froebel Certificates have recently been re-established at Roehampton University and are developing in Edinburgh ... the next generation of Froebelians is emerging, trained, in the practical apprenticeship way, in reflective practice through in-service training. (2011, p. 64)

Montessori put forward the notion of different 'Planes' or stages through which young children progress. It was during the first Plane (0 to 6 years) that Montessori saw children as developing their abilities in such important areas as short-term memory, and spoken or expressive language, and receptive language or the ability to receive instructions, questions and directions, and respond to these with understanding. Montessori believed that it was during this first Plane that adults working with young children typically see the greatest steps in learning taking place. Here, we can take this notion of 'seeing' steps in learning and link it directly to the earlier definition provided by Daudelin (1996) at the beginning of this chapter. Let us now look more closely at this stage and link Montessori's theoretical view to the realities found in actual practice. By doing so, it is possible to explore our own thinking and practice in direct relation to one approach that is considered by many to be successful.

Within the first Plane, Montessori identified 11 'sensitive' periods during this stage, which practitioners can use as a framework for engaging in critical reflection of young children. Actively engaging with parents about their child's behaviours during this period can offer early years practitioners invaluable insights regarding early cognitive development, motor coordination and social skills as well as other important factors such as the quality of early attachment (Herbert, 2005; Pearce,

2009). During this period, from birth to around 12 months, children are developing their ability to crawl and walk. They are also exploring their environment through touching, grasping and holding objects, and moving. Others have recognized the importance of these physical and sensory activities for some time and have built these activities into their work with children. Goddard Blythe (2008, p. 140), cited in Miller and Pound (2011, p. 90), have, for example, commented:

> The Steiner Waldorf curriculum focuses on the ability of young children to learn through imitation and through activity. Movement facilitates integration of sensory experience … Actions carried out in space help us literally to 'make sense' of what we see. Sight combined with balance, movement, hearing, touch and proprioception … help to integrate sensory experience and can only take place as a result of action and practice.

It is during this first stage or Plane that young children between the ages of 1 and 4 can also be observed to fixate upon particular objects and detail. This is an important element in their development because they are acquiring attention and concentration as well as developing their visual skills and internally representing visual features such as contours and shapes within the brain. In addition, and of equal importance, is the fact that by fixating on objects young children are also engaging in a process of verbal mediation whereby they attach verbal utterances and labels to these objects. The effective practitioner will observe young children fixating upon objects and will focus and reflect upon the language the child uses and such other factors as the child's determination and concentration and their growing familiarity with particular objects and how they act upon these. During this period, the young child also progresses from making random sounds to babble, then words and phrases, followed by sentences, indicating an understanding of their own thoughts and ideas, and those of others.

Montessori also believed that in young children between the ages of 2 and 4 there can be observed a need for consistency and a desire for sameness. The emphasis for professionals working with young children at this sensitive period would appear very obvious in that they would need to pay very careful attention to the environments they create during this period. Some children can become distressed when their environments are radically changed. During this period, young children appear to respond well to routines. Again, the professional practitioner might reflect upon the importance of regular and established routines both at home and in the classroom and how young children, particularly those from homes where there is much chaos and disorganization, must adapt.

Montessori thought that between the ages of 2 and 6 children appear to demonstrate a natural interest in elements of music, such as beat, rhythm and singing. 'Grace and Courtesy' and 'Refinement of the Senses', which might appear to us to be outdated concepts, can also, Montessori suggested, be observed during this stage. Here, the young child aged between 2 and 6 imitates those positive and considered behaviour patterns of others, which facilitates the internalization of these behaviour types into their own schema, and at around 3 to 4 years of age become absorbed by sensory stimuli such as touch and taste. Other factors that Montessori identified during this stage were:

- an apparent fascination with writing where the young child at around 3 to 4 years of age can be observed trying to copy letters and words or numbers and symbols
- an interest in reading where the young child between 3 and 5 years of age can be observed to display interest in the sounds of letters and words
- an interest in spatial relationships between 4 and 6 years of age where the young child internally represents relationships between objects and their immediate environments.
- a development of basic concepts in mathematical thinking using concrete materials between 4 and 6 years of age.

It is then during the second Plane that the curriculum begins to reflect the type of curriculum more commonly found in the majority of state primary schools and it is during this stage that the child's learning and thinking become more abstract in nature. In a sense, therefore, the child is at a stage where they are going beyond simply reacting to sensory stimuli within their immediate environments. These ideas have close similarities to those of Bruner's *Symbolic* mode referred to in Chapter 7. More formalized learning becomes apparent at this stage.

Independence, and the ability to look after oneself, are also key features of this philosophy. In Montessori nurseries, for example, children are encouraged to engage with such tasks as putting on their clothes and tidying up, which assist in their own development and contribute to their immediate communities. Montessori teachers also stress the importance of children developing at their own pace, and they encourage children to internalize at a very young age the notion that learning is something to be embraced and enjoyed. What then are the implications for young children who experience difficulties in these areas because of poor coordination or because they have never been taught by their parents or caregivers to engage in these activities at home?

Repetition of tasks is another important feature of the Montessori Method as this works to underpin the foundations of future abstract reasoning. There is an important distinction to be made here, however, in that new skills are not taught through an uninteresting repetition of activities but through the creative over-learning of exercises that facilitate and prepare the child to internalize new concepts and new understanding. When new concepts are introduced to the child, a three-step process is used, namely, introducing the new idea, comprehending it in concrete terms and finally comprehending it in abstract terms. Teaching and learning are very individualized for each child and the Montessori Method places great emphasis upon observation skills that are developed through the five senses.

It is interesting at this point to reflect upon how Montessori's ideas 'fit' with the current requirements of the Early Years Foundation Stage (EYFS) and the educational philosophies supported and espoused by the government in the UK. Though similar, there are significant differences, perhaps most notably, for example, in the way children's progress is assessed and recorded. In addressing this particular point, Miller and Pound have drawn attention to the fact that advocates of the Montessori principles have worked closely with the Office for Standards in Education (Ofsted) in the UK and with local authorities to encourage the use of approaches based upon these principles and, in turn, it has been recognized that these principles lead to sound and effective practice:

> In 2008, 88% of Montessori nurseries were considered by Ofsted to be 'outstanding' or 'good'. Concerns remain that local authorities have the power to oversee EYFS provision and to monitor its quality when assessing nurseries' eligibility for state funding for 3- and 4-year-olds' places. Interpretations of the EYFS can vary from one local authority to another and … can easily ignore the particular nature of Montessori education. (2011, p. 31)

However, Miller and Pound have also called for caution:

> External pressures from government guidance or a management hierarchy can lead practitioners to focus on curriculum 'delivery' or 'coverage' as the main focus of their practice. Such a view would have been anathema to the foundational theorists … but in England it has become a feature of the Early Years Foundation Stage (EYFS) (DfES, 2008) and the National Curriculum in primary schools, causing uncertainty for many practitioners. (2011, p. 165)

It is also worth noting that those who have trained to work as Montessori teachers are not eligible to work as teachers in state schools in the UK.

Exercise

How does a knowledge and understanding of different theoretical perspectives support practitioners in developing effective practice with young children?

Why might it be important for early years practitioners to adopt belief systems that emphasize potential as opposed to ability?

Why is it important for young children to learn how to learn and what role can early years practitioners play in facilitating this?

Summary

This chapter has brought together the concepts of learning and reflection that underpin good practice in early years and primary school settings. Key factors in developing young learners and the importance of creating purposeful and meaningful environments were explored in relation to a number of theorists and key figures who have influenced our thinking and who have provided us with the necessary foundations and landscape to further explore our practice both now and in the future.

As we move into the second decade of the twenty-first century, it is worth considering how differing theoretical perspectives and our interpretation of these might influence professional practice in the future. To do so would be to engage at an even deeper level of critical reflection. Our societies and communities, and the way in which we choose to educate our children, will change dramatically over our own life times as has been the case in recent generations. Changes in technology, political policy and, perhaps most importantly as Bruner might suggest, culture will have an enormous impact upon the learning and development of our children and young people in the forthcoming decades.

RECOMMENDED READING

Alexander, R. (ed.) (2010). *Children, their World, their Education: Final Report and Recommendations of the Cambridge Primary Review*. Abingdon: Routledge.

An up-to-date review of the current situation regarding primary education gained from extensive consultation.

Department for Education and Skills (DfES) (2008). *Statutory Framework for the Early Years Foundation Stage*. Nottingham: DfES Publications.

A necessary piece of reading for all practitioners working with children in the early years.

Montessori Schools Association/DCSF (2008). *Guide to the Early Years Foundation Stage in Montessori Settings*. London: Montessori St Nicholas/DCSF.

A very useful reference for practitioners wishing to gain a much greater understanding of the work undertaken by Montessori practitioners, and the principles that underpin such work.

REFERENCES

Brown, E. (1999). *Loss, Change and Grief*. London: David Fulton.
Buckingham, D. (2000). *After the Death of Childhood: Growing up in the Age of Electronic Media*. Cambridge: Polity Press.

Burden, R.L. (1987). Feuerstein's instrumental enrichment programme: important issues in research and evaluation. *European Journal of Psychology of Education, 2, 1,* 3–16.

Daudelin, M. (1996). Learning from experience through reflection. *Dynamics, 24, 3,* 36–48.

Department for Children, Schools and Families (DCSF) (2008). *Special Educational Needs in England.* London: DCSF.

Dowling, M. (2005). *Young Children's Personal, Social and Emotional Development.* London: Paul Chapman Publishing.

Feez, S. (2010). *Montessori and Early Childhood.* London: Sage.

Fenton, B. (2006). Junk culture 'is poisoning our children'. *Daily Telegraph,* 12 September, p. 1.

Feuerstein, R., Rand, Y. & Hoffman, M.B. (1979). *The Dynamic Assessment of Retarded Performers: The Learning Assessment Potential Device, Theory, Instruments and Techniques.* Baltimore, MD: University Park Press.

Feuerstein, R.R., and, Y., Hoffman, M. & Miller, R. (1980). *Instrumental Enrichment.* Baltimore, MD: University Park Press.

Goddard Blythe, S. (2008). *What Babies and Children Really Need.* Stroud: Hawthorn Press.

Herbert, M. (2005). *Developmental Problems of Childhood and Adolescence.* London: BPS/Blackwell.

Holland, J. (2001). *Understanding Children's Experiences of Parental Bereavement.* London: Jessica Kingsley.

Johnson, J. (2010). *Positive and Trusting Relationships with Children in Early Years Settings.* Exeter: Learning Matters.

Kellet, M. (2010). *Rethinking Children and Research: Attitudes in Contemporary Society.* London: Continuum Publishing.

MacBlain, S.F. & MacBlain, M.S. (2004). Addressing the needs of lone-parent pupils, *Academic Exchange Quarterly, 8, 2,* 221–5.

MacBlain, S.F. & Purdy, N. (2011). Confidence or confusion: how prepared are today's NQTs to meet the additional needs of children in schools? *Journal of Teacher Development, 15, 3.*

Mayall, B. (2002). *Towards a Sociology for Childhood: Thinking from Children's Lives.* Maidenhead: Open University Press.

Miller, L. & Pound, L. (2011). *Theories and Approaches to Learning in the Early Years.* London: Sage.

National Statistics (2003). *Social Trends.* London: Stationery Office Books.

Palmer, S. (2006). *Toxic Childhood.* London: Orion Books.

Pearce, C. (2009). *A Short Introduction to Attachment and Attachment Disorder.* London: Jessica Kingsley.

Pugh, G. & Duffy, B. (eds) (2006). *Contemporary Issues in the Early Years.* London: Sage.

QCA (2000). *Curriculum Guidance for the Foundation Stage.* London: QCA.

Schön, D.A. (1987). *Educating the Reflective Practitioner.* San Francisco, CA: Jossey-Bass.

Wells, R. (1988). *Helping Children Cope with Grief.* London: Sheldon.

Zwozdiak-Myers, P. (ed.) (2007). *Childhood and Youth Studies.* Exeter: Learning Matters.

GLOSSARY OF TERMS

Accommodation: This involves changing or adapting an existing schema, concept or idea to embrace new knowledge. Piaget believed that children learn by adaptation, which includes assimilation and accommodation.

Animistic thinking: The pre-operational child ascribes feelings to objects.

Assimilation: According to Piaget, 'assimilation is the integration of external elements into evolving or completed structures' (Piaget, 1970, p. 706). By this he means that new information is added into existing schemas or categories. Assimilation is an active and selective process.

Association: A relationship between two or more events.

Asymmetric relationship: A relationship which fosters the transfer of knowledge from a more knowledgeable peer to a less experienced learner.

Autism: A complex developmental disability that typically appears during the first three years of life and is the result of a neurological disorder that affects the normal functioning of the brain, impacting development in the areas of social interaction and communication skills. Both children and adults with autism typically show difficulties in verbal and non-verbal communication, social interaction and leisure or play activities.

Behavourism: A learning theory that focuses on objectively observable behaviours and discounts activities of the mind – how a child thinks, feels or interprets an event.

Behaviour theorists: These include Watson, Skinner and Thorndike, amongst others. Although Pavlov is often included as a behaviourist, he was a physiologist who described one aspect of learning.

Classical conditioning: A learning process that occurs when an association develops between two events, sometimes after one or multiple pairings, and becomes fixed in a person's mind. For example, a child is sick on a long car journey. In future, the same child may become distressed at the thought of a car journey for fear of being sick. Mum gets a toddler's wellies ready to take to the park. She may have to repeat this a number of times before her toddler, on seeing the boots, makes an association between the wellies and the park.

Cognition: A broad term which includes, amongst other things, mental processes such as attention, perception, language, thinking and problem solving.

Cognitive development: The development of internal mental processes.

Computer assisted learning: Skinner developed computer programmes to teach skills such as arithmetic and spelling, based on operant conditioning.

Conditioned stimulus (CS): Previously neutral, a stimulus which now elicits a response. For example, you see the McDonalds's sign and then catch a whiff which reminds you that you are hungry. When you next see the McDonalds's sign, your mouth might start to water or your tummy rumble.

Conservation: The principle that quantities remain constant regardless of changes to their appearance.

Constructivism: A theory of knowledge (epistemology) that argues that humans generate knowledge and meaning from an interaction between their experiences and their ideas.

Cultural tools: The products of human, cultural and historical activity.

Culture: This is a complex concept. Put simply, it involves the socially transmitted behaviour patterns, arts and beliefs passed from one generation to another.

Egocentrism: An inability on the part of a child in the pre-operational stage of development to see any point of view other than their own. For example, Jamie is playing hide and seek with his granny. To hide, he covers his eyes assuming that if he can't see then he can't be seen.

Equilibration: This involves the child finding a balance between external (environmental) and internal thinking processes. Disequilibration is the result of a mismatch between the two.

Extinction: A reduction and eventual cessation of a behaviour in the absence of a reinforcer.

Generalization: Where a response generalizes to similar stimuli. For example, Little Albert generalized his fear of a white rabbit to cotton wool and white beards.

Higher order thinking: This includes logical and abstract thinking, ordering, classifying, etc.

Horizontal decalage: The term used by Piaget to describe inconsistent performance on tasks involving similar mental operations.

Interpsychological: When information is transmitted between the child and others, including their parents, family, peers and early years professionals.

Intrapsychological: When the child internalizes knowledge gained from their experience with others.

Latent: Stored learning that is not immediately observable until a specific reinforcer or incentive is presented. For example, your friend drives you to college every day. You don't pay much attention to the route until she is ill and you have to drive yourself.

Law of Effect: Thorndike believed that actions are repeated for positive rewards and disappear when rewards are not repeated.

Learning: This is the permanent acquisition of knowledge or a skill.

Lower order thinking: This involves innate factors including perception, attention and memory.

Meaningful event or happening: Lessons are centred on events which are highly meaningful to the child and touch their emotions. Subsequently, each lesson follows a plot relating directly to an event.

Mediated learning: According to Vygotsky, the interaction between the child and their environment is not immediate. Instead it is mediated through cultural tools (language, art, music, etc.), psychological tools (mental processes) and social tools (social interaction).

Negative reinforcer: Use of time out or the naughty step, loss of privileges such as sweets/television, etc.

Neo-Piagetians: A group of researchers who sought to develop and refine Piaget's theory.

Operant conditioning/instrumental conditioning: This is also referred to as instrumental conditioning and is learning which occurs when a behaviour is either rewarded or punished. Through operant conditioning an association is made between a behaviour and a consequence of that behaviour.

Peer tutoring: A learner who mentors or tutors another.

Peers: A group of children who spend time together on a daily basis.

Perestroika: The policy of reconstructing a series of political and economic reforms in the former Soviet Union under the leadership of Mikhail Gorbachev which encouraged trade between Russia and non-Marxist countries.

Phobia: According to the American Psychiatric Association, a phobia is an irrational and excessive fear of an object or situation. In most cases, the phobia involves a sense of endangerment or a fear of harm.

Positive reinforcer: Use of praise, rewards, attention, money, star charts, etc.

Punishment: This varies in severity and length and may include the use of time out or the naughty step, the withdrawal of privileges, a ticking off, a severe scolding, a smack, etc.

Reinforcement schedule: The probability that behaviour will receive a reinforcer. Skinner identified four reinforcement schedules: a continuous reward is given every time the behaviour is displayed; with a fixed ratio, a reinforcer is given at set intervals, for example every third or fourth time; a fixed interval occurs at a specific time, for example every 5 minutes; with an intermittent or variable schedule, rewards/ reinforcers are offered at differing times. The latter offers the most effective type of reinforcement.

Rigidity of thought: The child's inability to reverse sequences and their inability to adjust to changes in appearance.

Rote learning: The focus here is on committing facts to memory rather than on understanding.

Scaffolding: A metaphor coined by Wood, Bruner and Ross (1976) to describe the support that people need in learning new skills.

Scheme/schema: Piaget used the term scheme, most often referred to as a schema, to describe the basic unit of intelligent behaviour. It is an active process. Schemas are not fixed but evolve and develop with experience.

Semiotic: The study and general theory of signs and symbols in languages, and their relationship to the things they represent, to each other, and their use.

Social constructivism: Social constructivism emphasizes the importance of culture and context in understanding what occurs in society and constructing knowledge based on this understanding (Pagram and McMahon, 1997).

Spontaneous recovery: This is the re-occurrence of a classically conditioned response after extinction has occurred.

Stimulus: An action or event that triggers a reaction. For example, if a teat is placed at the side of a baby's mouth, the baby will instinctively suck; the smell of food may cause your mouth to water; or you may find yourself humming along to a favourite tune.

Symbolic: One object representing another – for example, a cardboard box represents a car.

Symmetric: A relationship which includes peers who bring the same level of knowledge to problem solving.

Systematic desensitization: This works on the principle that fear triggered, for example, upon seeing a spider can be reversed or unlearned. The person is first taught relaxation exercises, and then shown a picture of their feared object (such as a spider). Over a period of time they are introduced to a real spider. It is believed that relaxation will cancel out fear.

Unconditioned stimulus (UCS): A stimulus that naturally and automically elicits a response. For example, hearing the theme tune of a favourite programme may cause a child to come running to watch.

Zone of proximal development (ZPD): The distance between a child's actual developmental level, as determined by independent problem solving, and the level of potential development as determined through problem solving under adult guidance or in collaboration with more competent peers (Vygotsky, 1978, p. 86, cited in Wertsch, 1985)

INDEX

Added to a page number 'f' denotes a figure, 'g' denotes glossary and 't' denotes a table.